ADVANCE PRAISE FOR *FROM ZERO TO FAITH*

"As the consummate professional and as an outstanding business partner Brenda as a mentor, friend, role model and spiritual coach has guided me to understand faith as a way of life and as a source of strength, inspiration, innovation and transformation in fulfilling my business endeavors."

~Astrid Chirinos
Founder & CEO, Diverso Global Strategies

"I have been moved and inspired by Brenda's story. Her courage in being so open about the path she has taken is so refreshing. Specifically, it is helpful to 'hear' her thought process as she both re-creates for the reader the path she has taken, and also teases out the key lessons that we can incorporate into our own lives and business plans."

~Chelvanaya B. Gabriel
CTO, Westry Wingate Group, Inc.

From Zero To Faith

Real Talk for Real Business!
(The Story No One Will Tell You)

Brenda F. Anderson

CENTERING PRESS

CENTERING PRESS
an imprint of Westry Wingate Group, Inc.

Cover Design by Julio Colmenares, CGR Creative

Westry Wingate Group, Inc.
http://www.wwgpress.com

ISBN-13: 978-1-935323-09-9
ISBN-10:   1-935323-09-1

My Prayer of Jabez

God bless me indeed! Bless my family and my businesses!

Grow me spiritually and faithfully, increase my finances and my financial security. Grow me emotionally, preparing me for love and for marriage.

Keep your hand upon me, my family and my businesses. Let our work and actions continue to be a reflection of you. Let the words of my mouth and the meditation of my heart be acceptable in thy sight and let no weapons formed against me, my family and my businesses prosper.

Protect me, my family and my businesses from evil, harm and danger and let nothing befall us that will keep us from doing your will ... in the name of Jesus I pray ... Amen!

TEN LESSONS

FROM ZERO TO FAITH

INTRODUCTION

If you know the story of Jabez from the Bible, you will understand that his story does not reveal much about him. What we learn in the brief reference (I Chronicles 4) about the man is that he had faith that whatever happened to him would only be temporary. He also believed that there was something unique about his life that entitled him to believe that something better was in store for him.

So, from the moment I began my journey as an entrepreneur, I adapted Jabez' prayer as my daily prayer, meditation and reflection of my faith.

I first read Bruce Wilkinson's book *The Prayer of Jabez* in 2001. I don't think it was simply a coincidence that this happened to be the same year that I started my first business. Although I have never met Bruce, I knew as I read his book that the messages from the pages of *The Prayer of Jabez* were written with me in mind. Not that Bruce wrote the book for me, he just revealed the story for me. For if I was going to understand why I was making this major decision for my life and the life of my family then I certainly would need a guide to help me understand what I was about to embark upon. I was destined to become an entrepreneur, and faith and prayer were to become the anchors of the foundation and blueprint of my business plan.

At the beginning, I asked myself a number of questions:

- Why am I doing this?
- What business management courses have I taken?
- What experience do I have with being an entrepreneur?
- More businesses fail than succeed - what is going to make my attempt successful?
- Most importantly, what business am I going to have?

For most observers, I was starting from zero. And yet, like Jabez, I had faith and believed that something better was in store for me. I believed with every fabric of my being that I was destined to move from a place of zero to faith.

Whether you are an experienced and/or successful entrepreneur or perhaps you are just beginning to put pen to paper to write your business plan, you have probably spent time engaged in very deep and introspective conversations just as I did when I started my business. Most of the personal conversations likely have brought you to a place in your journey of business ownership where you have also asked yourself, "Why am I doing this?"

Research reveals that most businesses started by entrepreneurs fail within the first three years. The International Franchise Association also reports that 84% of franchise owners said they worked harder than they expected to when they bought their franchise. Even higher numbers of aspiring entrepreneurs express surprise at the level of hard work required - so, why are you doing this?

Perhaps you decided to start a business because you were tired of working in a place in which you did not feel valued or there were no opportunities to grow. Maybe as today's economy continues to be filled with twists and uncertainty you are beginning to feel like you are sitting in the last seat of a roller coaster.

Better yet, perhaps you realized that you have a talent to produce or services to offer that are definitely needed by the marketplace. Of course, you may simply have woken up one morning and decided that there are more meaningful ways to provide for your family, your dreams or for yourself.

Business development research emphasizes that to start a new business of any kind is to be exposed to the risk of business failure; to start a business without financial resources or without a plan increases that risk. To start a business without understanding your purpose/destiny is starting at the negative side of zero, in other words, the risk is immeasurable.

I have written this book as a guide for the entrepreneurs or business owners whose business plans, financial resources and or actual businesses have taken them to a place where finding the answer to "Why am I doing this?" has become a daily test of faith. This guide will include real talk about business ownership. It will reveal some candid information that no one will tell you about the fears, pains and, yes, the joys of business ownership.

You may be asking at this point, "Why does Brenda believe she can help me answer the question of 'Why am I doing this?'" Or maybe you are asking me, "Why are you giving me the answers? Why are you doing this?" It is very simple: I understand my purpose! Although my destiny aligns with business ownership, business ownership is what I do; my purpose, however, is to help others understand their purpose.

As I have moved from a place of zero to faith, to a place where the best is still yet to come, I have had to travel a path of discovery. This path has led me to understand who I am, my being, my cause and what I stand for. To discover this understanding meant that I had to learn to experience life from the inside out and often from a place of feeling upside down.

The key objective of *From Zero To Faith* is to share the most important lessons I have learned regarding what creates misalignment in your business. More importantly, *From Zero To Faith* will help you discover how to make the necessary adjustments, or corrections, in order to ensure that your business is aligned with your purpose. This book will help you to understand the perils of not being aligned with your purpose or the purpose of your business. You will read about some lessons that I have learned. These lessons will tell a story that most business owners will not tell you.

From Zero To Faith is a guide designed for those who have faith that there is a higher calling for their work or businesses. This calling will help guide and inspire you toward your destiny/purpose. Whatever faith you may have, whatever religious or spiritual practice you follow, I encourage you to take time to answer the questions at the end of each lesson shared. Reflect on your responses, meditate, and use your responses as a guide for aligning and positioning your business for success.

LESSON ONE

FOCUS ON GOING NOT ON LEAVING TO FIND YOUR PURPOSE

And we know that all things work together for good to them that
love God, to them who are called according to His purpose.

ROMANS 8:28

It was November 2003 and I was standing in the middle of my kitchen crying. I had been in business for over two years at this point. As tears streamed down my face and formed small puddles in my open hands I began to weep uncontrollably.

"Where are you, God?" I pleaded in despair. "What am I doing wrong? What am I supposed to do, now?"

I asked these questions with the deepest belief that an answer would soon follow. Surely God could see the situation I was in. I was emotionally, intellectually, spiritually, physically and financially broke. My mortgage had not been paid in months and foreclosure was looming.

"Why then, God, am I here in this situation? I believe that this is what I am supposed to be doing. So why am I in this bad situation?"

And just like the despair that had overtaken me that November afternoon, a quiet peace of surrender began to engulf me, and in that peace came my answer: "You are not doing what you are supposed to 'be' doing - you are not aligned with your purpose!"

Perhaps as the owner of a business, or as an entrepreneur, you have reached a similar moment of despair where you felt you could not keep going. It may have appeared that everything you tried was not working and you found yourself asking, "Why am I doing this?"

It is the answer to this question that begins my first lesson. The answer to this all-consuming question will be found in your purpose. You will need to focus on going and not on leaving.

Lance Secretan of the Secretan Institute introduces us to the model "Why-Be-Do," his methodology for developing purpose-inspired leadership. The process begins with understanding your destiny, or why you are here on Earth. Can you honestly answer the question, "What is my purpose?"

Secretan shares insight on how often our purpose/destiny gets overshadowed by external influences, expectations, norms and values we refer to as socialization. Some socialization patterns take us down paths that lead us away from our purpose. As a result it is often very difficult to find our way back to our purpose or destiny. So we go through most of our lives living a rearview mirror existence. *If only ...*

I believe that my decision to embark on this thing called entrepreneurship was decided long before I realized that it was my destiny. Perhaps my decision to become an entrepreneur was planned before I was born or perhaps it was a "divine order."

To understand this concept of "divine order" you will have to understand more about my family. I come from a long family line of entrepreneurs. My father and most of my uncles and aunts were entrepreneurs. My grandfather, great grandfather and great, great parents were all entrepreneurs.

I am the youngest of seven children born to Luther and Mary B. Anderson. I was born in Columbus, a little metropolis city by the Chattahoochee River in west central Georgia. Of course, being born the youngest of seven was not so uncommon in the early 1950s. A unique feature of our family is that the seven of us were born generations apart.

My sisters - Mildred, Christine and Frances - are about twenty years older than I am. Some of their children, my nieces and nephews, are older than me, or only a few months younger than I am. Mildred and Chris always remind me of how embarrassed they were to be pregnant at the same time that our mother was pregnant with me.

My brothers - Robert, Luther and Tommy - are six to ten years older than me.

So when I came along, I was growing up pretty much as an only child. Of course, this gave me the most access to my parent's venture into business ownership.

However, my lineage of entrepreneurship began before my parents opened their business. Even today, when we all get together, my sisters and brothers reminisce about the adventures of working with my father as he developed his passion for business ownership. There are the stories of sitting on the back porch of our house before sunrise shelling peas and snapping green beans for my father to take to his personal customers. From what I understand, there were always bushels of peas and beans that needed to be shelled or snapped. It did not matter how many bushels, they had to be shelled or snapped before sunrise. The legacy of shelling peas and snapping beans eventually passed down to my brothers.

I can remember as a little girl wanting to be part of what looked liked a lot of fun - listening to my brothers as they swapped sport stories, shelled peas and snapped beans, all while sitting on the back porch before sunrise. This might be why I developed a love for sports, especially football and basketball.

My father's business venture did not end with just selling peas, beans, corn, sugarcane juice and syrup. He eventually decided that he could sell more if he had his own place to sell his goods. This decision was the beginning of my parents' grocery store business in 1956.

However, my fate and destiny as an entrepreneur goes back farther than my parents. My paternal grandfather, Charlie Anderson, died before I was born. Yet he was known to be an enterprising entrepreneur. In fact, my father's family roots are intertwined with what we now know as motor car sport racing in the United States. The history of this sport, I am told, goes back to taxes and alcohol laws. I will leave it at that since I promised my mother before she died to only tell this part of our family history when all parties involved had passed away. (I do, however, envision a great screen play for this story that needs to be told.)

The bottom line is that my paternal grandfather was killed testing the engine for a car that could potentially outrun the "revenuers." He and his brothers were known for modifying engines in the earlier version of the race car. This was their business. During a time when most Blacks did not have access to many of the rights we experience today, my grandfather and his brothers were very successful entrepreneurs. The story told is that Charlie was testing an engine that he and his brother had modified for a car. They wanted to see if the engine would perform well in the car, and make it faster. Apparently, my grandfather made two successful runs before the car collided with a bus. It is believed that he was killed instantly. I never met the man and yet, family members described him as being driven, innovative, enterprising, and "his own man." These are all critical competencies of any successful business owner that I have ever met. The ability to be your own person is fundamental to business ownership.

When I ask myself why I am operating a business, it is not just because my family history exposed me early in life to business ownership - I can say with confidence that I am supposed to be a business owner. Even without formal training or experience, my destiny/purpose is aligned with who I am, and what I am doing. Understanding your purpose is perhaps the most important part of being a successful entrepreneur/business owner. It is important to know that what you are doing is aligned with your purpose/ destiny. If you are unclear as to what your purpose is, then you will continue to find yourself struggling to answer the question: "Why am I doing this?" How can you be your "own person" when you don't know who that person really is supposed to be?

For most of us life is about what we can see or experience. It is about those tangible things we can count and measure and place a value on. So what happens when there is nothing to place value on? What happens when what you want to see is not there? What happens when what you experience is not what you wanted? Does life end or cease to exist? For some people when what they have learned is no longer their reality, they begin to feel as if the world or life as they know it is no longer worth the time. I discovered that when you are in this place you are not aligned with your purpose or your destiny. You have become someone or are doing something that does not connect you with your purpose. You are not your own person. Your spirit/ soul begins to feel empty. You can not be driven, innovative or enterprising when you are drifting!

The space in our lives that connects us to our destiny/purpose and to what we choose to do in life is our essence. This essence describes our character, our spirit or our soul. I discovered along the way of becoming a true business owner that my being, or what I stand for, is to help others find that connection between what they choose to do and their purpose.

Professionally, you might say that I am a consultant. In my work I say that I am a spiritual advisor. It is my purpose as a spiritual advisor to help others find the spirit within them that aligns them with their purpose and their vision as entrepreneurs. It is what I have learned, it is what God has shown me, and it is who I am. From a place of zero to a place of faith I am building my business and fulfilling my purpose at the same time.

In this book, I am sharing the experiences that provided me with the greatest lessons for becoming a purpose-inspired entrepreneur and business owner. The lessons I have learned in the process of building my business and embracing the spirit of my purpose have helped me to answer that question of why am I doing this. The process is what sustains me when the prospect of business is grim. It is what held me in place when I was not able to see how my business was going to survive. The process is what I hold onto when I have nothing to count, or to measure to tell me I am successful. It is that space I seek when the balance sheet or the profit and loss statement reflects a zero profit or a loss.

Through my discovery process I have learned some valuable lessons. One of those lessons is that I have a responsibility to teach others what I have learned. For the lessons I have learned have also helped me to make some very difficult decisions as I have accepted and embraced my purpose.

Some lessons learned in my discovery process have been extremely rewarding, while others have brought me to my knees in complete surrender. I have learned that you will continue to suffer disappointments and setbacks until you learn the lessons that your business or experiences are teaching you. Imagine reliving the same disappointments over and over again. You begin to question your abilities, your potential, as well as your faith. It is only when you are able to understand the lesson that you can successfully pass the test and move on to the next opportunity.

So where do we begin?

The first step begins with an assessment of your current reality. It does not matter where you are in your business ownership stage, it is always important to assess your current reality. To determine if you are ready to discover if you are aligned with your purpose/destiny in your business ownership, there are a few questions I encourage and invite you to answer.

Assessing Your Readiness for Discovery of Purpose

As I have learned, the resources and people you will need to help you with your business will be provided, especially if your business is aligned with your purpose/destiny. Evidence of this alignment is the opportunity I had when I met T. Falcon Napier and Linda Napier, developers of the ChangeWorks! change management system. T and Linda were introduced to me by a business associate who I had met only a few months prior to finishing this book.

As a result of meeting them, I became a certified ChangeWorks! practitioner. Why is this important to you? The ChangeWorks! system was one missing piece that I needed in order to help others to understand how to determine if they and/or their business plans or strategies are aligned, or in "flow," with their purposes.

Before continuing, I encourage you to glance at the ChangeGrid below, then use the table on the next page to evaluate and rate your perceived *Ability*, the perceived *Challenge*, and the perceived *Importance* for the following factors as it relates to your business or business plans. On a scale of 0-12, with 12 being the optimal rating, rate the activities listed for *Ability*, *Challenge* and *Importance*.

Figure 1: ChangeWorks! System ChangeGrid[1]

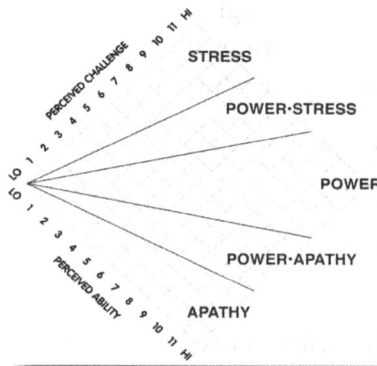

---

1   T. Falcon Napier & Associates, Inc. © 2009.

DESIRED OUTCOME: *A Successful Purpose-Inspired Business*

Key Activities	ABILITY	CHALLENGE	IMPORTANCE
1. Achieving the financial results you want for your business			
2. Developing a diversified profitable client base			
3. Implementing strategies that achieve the results you want for your business			
4. Selecting the right people or skills to achieve consistent results			
5. Finding your personal "sweet spot," or purpose			

It is important that you rate your responses based on your personal perception. Remember your perception is your reality. However, to determine what you can do about your responses, or your situation, you will want to know where your responses fall along the ChangeGrid, as shown in Figure 1.

The ChangeGrid determines your perspective or perception of your ability to do something about your answers, or situation. It also determines your perception of the degree of challenge it is for you to do something about your answers. Lastly, the ChangeGrid reflects your perception of the level of importance of doing something about your answers or situation.

The ChangeGrid is the result of nearly 30 years of research and development and incorporates the insights of over 400 models of human behavior dating back over 2000 years. It reveals the likelihood of someone actually following through on activities or tasks. It also indicates how much and what type of support an individual will need to get back on track and aligned for reaching their goals or desired outcomes.[2]

We will discuss your responses and current reality based on your perceptions and the ChangeGrid later in Lesson Nine. This book was developed to help you understand the importance of aligning your business

---

2   T. Falcon Napier & Associates, Inc. © 2009.

with your purpose. The ChangeGrid is an excellent tool that works much like the x-ray process - it will help you to see and understand more about what you are doing that might be misaligned with your purpose. Information to learn more about obtaining your personal ChangeGrid can be found at http://www.galileeagency.com.

As I have shared, I come from a long line of entrepreneurs. However, I felt early on in my professional ambitions that I could be more successful and certainly avoid some of the hardships that my parents experienced if I pursued my education and career in either the entertainment industry or in law. Early in my educational pursuits these were my plans and the course I followed. As the youngest of seven children I also always felt that I needed to demonstrate my worthiness to the family by excelling in whatever I did. But I always found myself daydreaming about owning my own business.

Although marriage and children directed me away from my goals of going into entertainment and law early on, I moved quickly up the ranks in my corporate experience. Somewhere in my mid-30s I set a goal that I would start a business by the time I turned 50. I did not know what this business was going to do/produce, I just knew that I was going to have a business of my own. As Secretan relates, we can often hear that little voice in our heads reminding us of those goals we set early in our lives.

The little voice in my head kept getting louder as I continued up the corporate ladder.

"So when are you starting this business? You will be 50 years old in 10 years… 5 years… now only 2 years."

The voice began to almost speak in rhythm with the click of my heels as I walked from one endless meeting to another in the halls of Corporate America. The voice kept reminding me that I was not *being* what I was supposed to *be,* and I was not *doing* what I was supposed to be *doing.*

One night as I drove home late from my office, the voice in my head began to speak louder than the music playing on the car radio …

"You will be 50 years old in 2 years… It is time to go… When are you starting the business?"

It was as if the refrain from the familiar tune on the radio had been taken over by the voice playing in my head. I knew then that my daydreams were about to become a reality or the voice was only going to get louder!

I shared my dream with my family, friends and co-workers. Two of my friends who also worked with me at the large financial institution where I was employed at the time expressed a similar dream. They wanted to join me in making this dream a reality. I learned later, as I will share in Lesson 4, that although you may have similar dreams as others, no two individuals will have the exact same dream or the same purpose/destiny.

In 2000, my friends and potential business partners and I went to the mountains of Tennessee to develop our business plan. We were going to strategize on what we needed to do to build the business that we decided would be a consulting organization. When we came from the mountains I decided that I would be the one to leave my position and benefits behind to begin the company we had developed on paper. As my daydreams began to transform into a reality, my passion for the work I was doing in my role at the financial institution was waning.

This phenomenon is the beginning of the first lesson that I want to share with you. I learned that when you focus on where you are going, there is very little space in your life for focusing on where you are, or what you need to leave. Here begins a very simple two-part lesson:

You can not go unless you move.
When you focus on going, you must not focus on leaving.

When you focus on leaving there will always be a part of you that will want you to stay where it is safe and where the environment is known. Moving toward the unknown can be very frightening. If you are not focused on where you are going, it becomes very difficult to move. The concept of leaving implies that there is something you must leave behind. When you decide to go toward a new place, your focus can not be on what is left behind, it must be focused on what lies ahead or where you are going.

This is an important part of understanding your calling or purpose. Think of a situation when someone familiar who you have not seen for a while is calling your name in a crowd. Or perhaps your child has become separated from you in the mall. When you hear your name called and that familiar voice calling, you tend to turn toward the caller - you tend not to focus on the situation or the crowd that may be surrounding you. Your focus will only be on how you will get to whomever is calling you. This is how your destiny/purpose calls you. You will recognize the familiarity of the call and you will begin to understand that you must find a way to get to that call!

When I decided to pursue starting a business, there were several factors that could have prevented me from listening to my calling. At the time, I had been a single parent for over 18 years and my youngest son, Rashad, was in his second year at Morehouse College in Atlanta. I had two mortgages on my house and other financial liabilities. I had a very good job and had successfully implemented two internationally recognized projects for the corporation. However, my purpose was calling and I knew I had to answer - I had to move in order to go. I knew that what I needed to do must be aligned with my purpose and my spirit.

As Secretan illustrated, my "why (*destiny*) - be (*cause*) - do (*calling*)"[3] had to be aligned in order for me to truly experience a purpose-inspired life. I left my position with the corporation in 2001 and decided to dedicate my focus on building the business. This was when and where I decided to go.

Regardless of what business you decide to start or what business you are leading, as an entrepreneur it is important to answer the following questions: Does my business align with my purpose and my being? Am I doing what I am supposed to be doing?

The Galilee Agency was founded in February 2001. In the United States, 2001 proved to be a challenging year for most businesses, large and small, new or established. By late 2001, it was apparent that my focus on the calling of the business was stronger than that of the other owners. We agreed that since I was the only one in a position to respond to the calling, I needed to become the sole owner of the company.

This was probably the most difficult decision I have had to make since starting the business. These were my friends and business partners and now we had to sign papers to redefine our relationship. However, it was the only way I could *go* - I had to focus on the "calling" and not on the leaving.

---

3   Secretan, Lance H. K. Inspire! What Great Leaders Do. Hoboken, N.J.: John Wiley, 2004.

I can say with certainty that there will be some tough decisions that you will need to make as an entrepreneur or business owner. Some of those decisions will mean "leaving" some people behind or out of your plans to go in a new or different direction. You will need to focus on going and not on leaving in order to find the purpose in your decision.

For two years I worked tirelessly trying to establish The Galilee Agency. Every success was followed by a disappointment. By late 2003 my well-established credit rating was destroyed and creditors' calls outnumbered calls from potential clients, family and friends. As I struggled to keep ahead of foreclosure on my home, I asked those challenging questions:

"Why am I doing this? Where are my friends? Where are the people I've helped along the way?"

I still marvel sometimes at the fact that in my position with my former employer, I was often sought out by others for coaching and direction in addressing career challenges and opportunities. Since deciding to go two years earlier, not one of those individuals ever reached out to me to offer a potential opportunity or even an encouraging word.

As I wallowed in my despair that November in 2003, I turned to my faith and to God and asked Him, "Why am I doing this? What am I doing wrong? Have you forsaken me?"

It was God's answer to my questions that helped me to understand that what I was doing was not aligned with my purpose. My spirit was depressed or was broken because my work was not aligned with my purpose. To keep the doors open and the creditors at bay, I had begun to accept business that had nothing to do with my mission, purpose or calling. It was more about making money than fulfilling purpose. Yet I was unable to get traction for or sustain the business. The work was far from rewarding and my spirit was broken.

I was to learn later that when your passion is missing in what you are doing, it is a strong indicator that your work or what you are doing is not aligned with your purpose. When your spirit feels compressed, twisted, drained, anxious, dejected or just plain empty, you are not aligned with your purpose and, therefore, your work will not reward you spiritually, economically or in any capacity. I realized in my efforts to survive financially my work was not purposeful.

So how was it that I discovered that what I am now doing is aligned with my purpose? To understand this will allow me to tell you more about the type of business I am in and the work that I do. For industry classification my work is considered business consulting. The consulting is, however, primarily focused on the practice of organizational development and human performance. The types of services I provide include leadership and employee development, coaching, training, organizational development and process design. I work with organizations to help them develop the capacity for solutions to ensure that they get the type of results they want. What makes the services of The Galilee Agency unique is that we work with both people and process solutions. This may not sound unique, however, in most organizations individuals who have the primary responsibility for managing processes designed to deliver services, products or results are typically not the same individuals responsible for managing processes designed to develop people.

This was apparent when I came to work in 1994 for my former employer. Before joining my former organization, I had spent the prior ten years working for another well-known financial organization. This organization had engaged in a process in the mid-1980s much like other American organizations who were trying to stay ahead of the Japanese quality improvement movement. It was evident that the budding of the new global economy was having an impact on American ingenuity. Companies like my employer in the 1980s were working on finding ways to ensure that they remained relevant and globally competitive. Our organization decided to follow a dual level approach.

One approach focused on process improvement and the other approach focused on what we referred to as people skills training. The people skills training was led by the human resources organization while the process improvement effort was led by key leaders from the top levels of sales, underwriting, operations and marketing. As with most efforts like this, much of the focus and resources were assigned to the process improvement approach. The people skills training was designed for a four-hour session while the process training covered a 12-week period. The process training also had significant reporting and follow-up assignments that made the message clear that this was a business imperative for the organization.

As Division Manager for Training and Development in my region, I was one of the few individuals who were selected to be a Quality Administrator in the organization. This meant that I led both the people and process efforts. Most regions had individuals from Human Resources assigned to the people side of the work while other individuals from operations, underwriting or sales led the process efforts. As I now understand my purpose, it was not an accident that I had been selected to be a Regional Quality Administrator. With responsibility for both approaches I began to develop models to help manage the work efficiently. As I brought the efforts together I realized that when people are aligned with the process, they tend to perform more effectively.

So when I decided to move to Charlotte and join my new employer, there was a quandary as to where I would best fit. I had substantial training experience as well as certifications that indicated that I would be a valuable asset in the training department of human resources. However, I also had substantial operations management experience with quality improvement and process management certifications. In fact my offer letter indicated that I was to be an Assistant Vice President responsible for Management/ Leadership Development and Quality Improvement Process. The print shop refused to put all of my title on my business cards. We eventually agreed to an abbreviation that would capture the "essence" of who I was to become – a "MLD/QIP" consultant!

For most of my associates, I was an anomaly. They wanted to understand my methodology and some even questioned if I knew what I was doing. Those questions quickly subsided when my results began to speak for themselves.

As I continued to work for the organization, I continued to take on roles that did not fit neatly into a department. In fact, my last boss in the e-commerce division just created a title – just as had been done at the beginning of my tenure with the organization. I was responsible for aligning people and process in order to deliver results. One project involved developing the first Spanish language website for the organization to promote our consumer products to the Spanish speaking customer. At the same time I was also leading a project focused on closing the digital divide in lower wealth communities in our footprint.

So when I started The Galilee Agency I knew that my work would involve aligning people and processes in order to deliver results. As an organizational development consultant, most of the work engagements for The Galilee Agency involve these types of focus. However, to align people with process, it is important that processes are aligned with the organization's mission and vision. The space between an organization's mission and vision is often what we refer to as organizational culture or "essence." It is that space where norms, values, policies and procedures exist. As process consultants, when we go into organizations that are struggling to achieve results, we can identify areas of misalignment. In other words, when the "real" culture does not align with the organization's mission/purpose, it will be very difficult to align people with process.

As I have worked with organizational and business leaders, it became increasingly apparent to me when they were not aligned with their purposes. So in my process of discovering my purpose, I began to work with CEOs, Presidents and leaders of large and small organizations to help them align their visions with their purposes. As they became aligned with their purpose, they became more fulfilled and inspired. In most cases these individuals increased their capacity to achieve the results they wanted, even exceeding their business goals and projections 95% of the time. In those situations where we did not achieve the goals there were often obvious situations of continuing misalignment and lack of readiness to go where the leaders or organizations needed to go. The pull to not leave what they were comfortable doing was just too great.

I have now incorporated this discovery process into my services. I call it "purpose-inspired" leadership coaching. From executives to business owners, as well as leaders at all levels of organizations, I fulfill my purpose by helping others discover their purpose.

It is important to know your calling and your purpose if you want your business to be truly fulfilling and rewarding. You may be in a place where you feel your business is not moving in the direction you want it to go or perhaps everything you are trying or have tried is not working. You feel stuck, conflicted and overwhelmed. You need to ask yourself: am I going in the right direction? Remember, you cannot go unless you move.

To move will mean that you must focus on going and not leaving. It will take some courage for you to go where you have never been or may not want to go. It will mean that you will need to make some difficult and tough decisions. Some of these decisions may require that you move away from those things that you thought were right or those people that make you comfortable. You will need to focus on going and not on leaving. In order to go you will need to move, and to move in the right direction you will need to understand your purpose or why you need to do what needs to be done.

Throughout this book, there will be questions to help you understand what needs to be done, through self-reflection and evaluation of your business, or business plans based on each of the book's ten lessons.

In the first of these worksheets that follows, you will see that your responses to the following questions will help to determine if your business/ work is aligned with your purpose.

LESSON ONE WORKSHEET
Focus On Going Not On Leaving To Find Your Purpose

1) Below, write your mission/purpose in life. What part of your mission speaks to your passion? If you do not know your mission/purpose, then what is it that you daydream or hope for over and over again?

2)   Describe an experience in life that brought you the greatest joy? How did you feel? What did you say about the experience? What did others say about the experience?

3) What words in your joyful description "pop" out from your experience? What do these words say about you?

Optional: Share your list of words with family & friends and ask them to tell you what type of individual they experience/see in your list of words.

4) What part of your business experiences/plans align with your list of words or what others have told you about your list? What words did you identify or did friends and family describe that do not align with your business experiences or plans?

5) Based on your responses to the questions in #4, are their areas of your business or business plans that may not be aligned with your mission? What are your plans to ensure that you are aligned with your mission/purpose? What plans will you need to put in place to ensure that you are moving and going toward the vision for your business?

Reflect, meditate on and/or pray about all of your responses.

Lesson Two

It Takes More Than Hope & Prayer: It Takes A Strong Foundation

Command those who are rich in this present world not to be arrogant
nor to put their hope in wealth, which is uncertain, but to put their
hope in God, who richly provides us with everything for our enjoyment.

TIMOTHY 6:17 (NIV)

Paul's letter to Timothy was to remind him that although wealth and money bring good things, it is more important to build your hope and foundation on those things provided by God. Although being in business is about making money, if this is the primary reason that you are in business then your business foundation will be built on uncertainty.

As we saw in Lesson One, it is important to understand your destiny/purpose and your calling. This is important as you begin to lay the foundation for building your business. It does not take a strong wind to blow down a structure without a sound and solid foundation. Regardless of what business you are building, it is important to begin with developing your foundation so that the framework will stand.

My parents' grocery business, "Anderson Grocery and Fruit Stand," started in the mid-1950s. It began with my father riding his bicycle to the farmer's market to buy fresh fruit and vegetables to sell to his co-workers at Golden Foundry and to the high wealth residents in Columbus, Georgia. I can still remember as a little girl riding up front in the large delivery basket of my father's bicycle. We would leave early Saturday mornings on a warm June day to make the five mile ride to the farmer's market down near the Chattahoochee River. I would help to pick out the melons, tomatoes and peaches. It was my task to find the best looking baskets offered by the southern peach farmers and to test their products.

Oh, to bite into one of those ripe Georgia peaches and have the juices run down my chin. This was proof that the basket had the best that the market could produce that morning. Product testing became one of my specialties as I imagined that juicy product becoming part of someone's homemade peach ice cream or warm peach cobbler. This is probably why I am a connoisseur of peach cobbler or anything made with peaches today. My product testing skills and craft eventually expanded into melons and other summer fruits.

When my father was able to buy an old truck we left the bicycle as back up for those days and times when his old army surplus truck would not start. It was up to my brothers and me to push the truck in order for it to start. My father was known at the market and by his faithful customers for the old smoking truck. We fondly named the truck "Putt, Putt Nellie Bell" for the smoke and noise it would make. Somewhere among the noise and smoke you could hear my father ringing a bell to let his waiting customers know we were there with their fresh fruit and vegetables. You could see the smoke before you could see the truck. Perhaps this was part of my father's marketing strategy and brand recognition campaign. All I know is that customers would be waiting wherever we decided to park the truck.

Eventually, a small fruit stand was added to my father's fleet. The stand was actually a small trailer that only two people could safely fit inside. Customers were served through a small window or from outside of the trailer. Cold nights in the trailer meant that store hours fluctuated according to how long we could tolerate the hard cold winter nights in the trailer without freezing to death. In the early days, I spent most nights with my mother in the fruit stand. My father continued to work at the foundry.

From the small trailer, my father expanded the facilities to a tin structure built on the property next to our home. The tin structure was often the target of neighborhood children throwing rocks against it. During the Georgia summer storms, we often did our version of "The Wizard of Oz" tornado scene. My mother became Auntie Em and I was Dorothy. As the strong storm winds whipped around us, we had to batten down the hatches and run for shelter.

From the tin structure, my father was able to build an actual brick and mortar structure that served the community for over 20 years. My mother, with a seventh grade education, was the General Manager, Accountant, Director of Customer Service and of Human Resources. My father, with

26

only a fifth grade education, was the Director of Business Development, Marketing, Sales and Operations. My parents built a relatively successful grocery business with their determination and faith. Access to capital and funding for business development was unheard of at that time for a business like ours.

When I reflected on my parents' business, I learned that my father made no decision without ensuring that his foundation was strong. He made sure that his products and services met the needs of his customers. He understood his customers and they respected him. He did not add any liabilities unless he knew he had the cash - there was no such thing as business financing for my parents. My father did not invest or buy anything until he was sure he could afford it, so he leveraged what he had in order to get what he needed.

My father's approach to business management is a lesson I wished I had remembered early in my business development. He understood that you can not have a sound business foundation if you take on any liabilities that you do not have assets to cover. The second lesson I learned is that developing a successful business takes more than hope and prayer, it takes a strong foundation. As Paul's letter to Timothy reminds us, do not put your hope in wealth for it is not guaranteed. In other words your foundation must be built on those assets that provide a balance for your business. Critical assets for a secure and strong foundation include your faith, your health, your family, good insurance, a good business plan, a unique value proposition and strong strategic relationships.

Early on in my business I hired an assistant to help with developing presentations and handling administrative responsibilities. She was a great spiritual support and helped with details that were outside my areas of expertise. Although she understood that the business was growing and clients were slow to come, it became more and more difficult to cover her salary and expenses. After awhile the burden of wondering how I was going to pay her kept me up most nights. The assistant realized my burden and spared me the agony. She went back to work full-time for our former employer after only a few months.

I started the business by setting up my office in my home. This worked well and perhaps was where I needed to have remained for the first five years of The Galilee Agency. For my business, most of my work is done with my clients in their locations. So when I decided to open an office with some other entrepreneurs, the business foundation was not secure enough to handle this financial liability. Although the rent was minimal it was still a liability that I did not absolutely need in the first five years of developing my business. Some of the most successful businesses were started in entrepreneur's homes.

Another critical factor for building a sound foundation is to know your unique value proposition. It is important that potential customers have a clear understanding of how what you provide can meet their needs or solve their problems. Communicating your message is as important as having a door that opens to your business. As with other liabilities, avoid costly marketing materials that do not communicate your message. A good professional looking business card, website and telephone message that clearly describes what you do are priceless in communicating your message.

Perhaps you have heard of the "elevator pitch"? An elevator pitch is designed to be shared with a potential customer during a elevator ride, or anywhere from 15 seconds to 3 minutes, and can be expanded to other situations. The elevator pitch is your opportunity to share your goals and intentions. You use it to describe your business with impact and conciseness - it is your "message." Your ability to communicate your message will determine your ability to communicate your unique value to your customers or potential customers.

My first business cards used a tagline: "Providing Solutions for the New Economy." Sounds good, if potential customers knew what solutions I provided. I spent money on cards and other materials that did little to realize business for me, not to mention that I spent money I did not have assets to cover. When you have limited assets, you need to ensure that any money you spend is going to make you money. Remember, money gets money and you don't make money unless someone understands your message.

In the early years, there were several other investments and financial liabilities that I took on that I did not have assets to cover. Perhaps one of the most significant liabilities was pursuing business that did not align with my business. We will discuss this in a later chapter. It took me two painful years before I was able to get my foundation in place to begin building my business. By this time, my credit rating and my financial resources were all but eradicated. It didn't matter that I had a good business plan with strategic objectives, goals and measures, what mattered was that I understood what was my unique value proposition and that money gets money. Although I was battered and bruised after two years, the lessons I learned helped me to be clear on my purpose and my message.

This is why it is so important to know what business structure will serve your business and your purpose well. There are lots of classes, written resources and free information that will help to guide you with this decision. It is important, however, to understand the legal protection you will need for your business. If you do not have an attorney or accountant, find a reputable one before you finish reading this page. Those legal and financial professionals that are reputable understand what you are about to embark upon and in most cases are willing to work with you to develop your business. (In most cases they have been where you are going.)

If you are a sole proprietor, ensure that your personal assets are completely separate from your business assets. If you decide to do a partnership, limited liability company (LLC) or otherwise, ensure that everyone understands how a liability may impact each partner.

Once you understand your business structure develop bylaws and other operating processes and policies to ensure that you have something to stand on in the event you run into difficulties. (This you can depend on: you will!) Evaluate the types of insurance that you will need to cover your services and/or products. A good insurance broker is also a good friend to have as one of your close business relationships.

Write a business plan - the content and details of the plan are determined by whether you will need to seek financial support. Some questions to answer in your plan may include the following:

- What will make customers want to do business with you versus any one else?
- What makes what you do unique?
- Do you know your competitors?
- Do you know of potential allies willing to help you?
- How will you get your message out about your business?

- What assets do you have that you will be able to leverage?
- What liabilities will you need to consider/anticipate?

It took a few difficult years to learn the lesson gained from these questions. It does not matter how much faith you have, you are going to have to work to make your business a reality. Faith without work and more work is death for your business.

Although I did a business plan and worked with my bank to secure funding, the message here is always: money gets money. Without assets to secure funding, the chance of getting funding from your financial institution is slim to impossible. With the recent economic environment and the impact it has had on lending, getting access to financing is reserved for the very few, and I mean very few. It is important to remember that if, for some reason, you use your home as collateral for financing and you run into financial challenges, then your financial institution now has claim to your home and your business.

Some entrepreneurs may be fortunate to have family members or close friends willing to support their business endeavors financially. Take caution here because, in most cases, when your financial supporters need their investment returned, you will probably not be in a position to make the return. This can get ugly fast - holidays become very uncomfortable when the money you borrowed from your uncle or grandmother is the family's only topic of conversation. Swallowing that last piece of pie at the family dinner becomes very difficult when you learn that Grandma put off her hip replacement because she loaned you money for your business and now you can't pay it back.

There are, of course, that unique breed of investors called "Angels." Just remember: "Angels are always with us." The same holds true for angel investors - once they invest, they become a part of your business and they are with you. You will need to decide how much of your business you are willing to give up in order to secure an investment from an angel and/or equity investor.

One of those assets that you may not consider necessary to ensure that you have a strong foundation, is your physical health. As a business owner or entrepreneur, you must learn to value your health. Take time to eat properly, get rest and take care of those things that can keep you going physically. Just as you rely on your car and other technology for your business, you will need to rely on your health for your business. If you are going to be in business, you will need to have the physical stamina to endure the long hours that will certainly be required of you. Although you may not be able to afford health insurance, you can not afford not to find resources to help you sustain your health. There are community clinics available who provide excellent healthcare services for nominal charges. Don't allow your pride prevent you from ensuring that your body and your health are secure. Your health is as important to sustaining a strong foundation as anything else you can invest in. It is very difficult to do business when you don't have your health to do it.

Another critical component for building a strong foundation is developing strong alliances and strategic relationships. Understanding this aspect of business development brought my business from the brinks of financial ruin.

One of the few friends I had during the early years was someone I had met while representing my former employer on an advisory board. She was the COO of a large community nonprofit organization. She valued my "free" counsel to help her in her role. Whenever she would see me at community events she would always ask how I was doing - not how was the business? but instead how was *I* doing?

During one of these events she asked how I was doing and invited me to have dinner with her soon. I followed up on the invitation the very next day. I knew that this was my opportunity to leverage this relationship. During dinner, I told my friend I needed to make money and I needed to do it within the next three months or I was going to be living on the streets. So I asked her to consider me for whatever opportunities she had in her organization. I also asked her for support in recommending me to other organizations.

Within three months I had two major contracts with new clients at the same time that I was coordinating a major project for the COO's organization. I began to build the foundation of my consulting business from these three engagements. It was the strategic relationship of someone who wanted to help me because I had helped her and her organization. I had invested in this relationship and had built social capital by developing a relationship based on faith, mutual respect and trust. From this relationship I was able to begin building the financial capital I needed to get traction to build my business.

You can hope that you will find customers or that customers will find you, your services or products. You will definitely find that prayer will help you to make it through the very lean times. And yet, it will take more than hope and prayer! It is essential that you build a strong foundation for your business if you want it to withstand the strong winds of uncertainty and adversity that are sure to blow your way.

LESSON TWO WORKSHEET
It Takes More Than Hope & Prayer:
It Takes A Strong Foundation

Is the foundation for your business secure? Answer the following questions to determine where there might be some cracks or areas requiring development/reinforcements.

1) What is the structure of your business? Will the business structure help you to achieve your personal and professional goals?

2) What is your unique value proposition? Why is your business different?

3) What do you want to have happen for your business? For you?

4) What are your assets? Will they cover your liabilities? What assurances or insurances do you have in place to strengthen the foundation of your business? How is your health? Is it an asset or liability?

5) Can you communicate or describe your business and what you do in 3 minutes? In 30 seconds? In 15 seconds? Share the speech with your supporters. Is your message clear?

[Develop an elevator pitch that you can share with a customer in the time it takes to travel three floors in an elevator.]

6) Who are your competitors and why are they your competitors? Who are your strategic alliances? What relationships do you have with them? How can these relationships help you with your business? .

Reflect, meditate on and/or pray about all of your responses.

Lesson Three

It Takes Money To Make Money

Feasting makes you happy and wine cheers you up, but you can't have either without money.

ECCLESIASTES 10:19

Even from the Old Testament, the value of money was fundamentally understood as a resource that provides more opportunity. Although having those things that give us immediate pleasure and satisfaction may provide for temporary happiness, we need to seek those resources that provide us with opportunities for sustaining pleasure and happiness.

As we saw in Lesson Two, more than hope and prayer are needed for a strong foundation - and that foundation will require money! I learned early on in developing my business that "money gets money." However, it is important to remember that it must be *your* money that is getting money. Whatever you choose as your measure of success for your business, money will be required. If you are not in business to make money, then you are not in business. Money coming in and money going out does not equate to making money. Making money means your money is making money, and you are making a profit.

Remember, however, if money is the only reason you are in business, then you will not be in business for long. Today's financial headlines remind us how greed and money-centered businesses ultimately unravel because their foundations are built on questionable principles and relationships.

For the first three years of my business, I was excited to just get business and clients! Many times I took on projects from clients who had limited resources and could not afford to pay me full value for my services. I would offer discounts and even do pro bono work with the hope that more work would follow. I soon learned that this was not the case. If potential customers or clients can not afford your services or products, then for the most part they are not your customers.

Be especially mindful of those who sometimes take advantage of other relationships they have with you! Thank them for the opportunity to discuss your services or products and let them know that when they can afford to pay for your services then you look forward to serving them.

This was a difficult lesson to learn. However, after understanding that "money makes money," I realized that making money was fundamental to my business. Even after it has been earned, there are those business owners who find asking for money to be a difficult proposition.

If asking for your earned money is difficult then you may want to ask if you truly believe in what you are doing. One of the primary reasons that individuals have problems asking for money is that they do not believe in the situation or principle in which the money represents. This is why understanding your purpose is so important to your business. If you understand that your business or what you are doing is aligned with your purpose/destiny, then asking for your work's value in money takes on a different meaning. It is not the money that you are asking for ... it is the value of your destiny!

Once you understand your value proposition, it is important to understand how that translates in the market place or with your potential customers. Set your prices and rates according to the needs of the marketplace. You will need to do your research to determine what is competitive and fair for your business or industry. Once you know this information then you must believe that your unique value proposition is worth the money.

The situation that brought this lesson to light for me involved an engagement I did for a former business associate. I had been recommended to an organization for some consulting work. I was asked to work with the leadership team to plan a large project. Again, I was hungry and desperate at the time and needed the engagement. After working on the project for a few months, it became obvious that I had not received payment for my work. I kept asking my contact on the project about the invoice that I had submitted three times. As each week passed, it became very uncomfortable for me to make the trip to the organization knowing that I had not received one dollar for my work.

One day, not sure if I was going to have enough gas to get home, I decided to stop by Accounting to determine what was happening with my payment. After searching for a half hour for the invoice, the Accounts Payable representative sheepishly admitted that my contact had not sent the invoice to Accounting for payment. I think the representative could hear the desperation in my voice. Since fate had it that I had a copy of the invoice with me, she agreed to take personal responsibility for expediting processing of the invoice.

The only way I got home on my empty gas tank that day was on the faith that Jabez had, knowing that the best was yet to come. The check arrived three days later.

The lesson here is to ensure that you have a billing or invoicing process that works for your business. Most organizations accept electronic invoices only. Even with this convenience, you will need to get comfortable with following up with your clients to ensure you get paid. What I have learned is that sometimes the larger the organization, the more difficult it can be to get paid. Large organizations process thousands of invoices per day with millions of dollars in account payables and account receivables. Accounts payable processes are often less customer focused and more focused on accuracy and cost savings for the organization.

After going almost 120 days before getting paid on a large account, I learned that I had to become more assertive in asking for my money. If you are fortunate to have someone in your business helping to manage your accounting, I recommend setting up some guidelines that will help that individual to understand that money makes money. In other words, it is important that everyone in your business understands that when your business gets paid, they get paid.

LESSON THREE WORKSHEET
It Takes Money to Make Money

Do your responses to the following questions reflect that you understand that it takes money to make money?

1)   Do you know the competitive market price for your business' products or services? What are your competitors' rates?

2)   Do you have an effective accounting process for invoicing and keeping track of account receivables and account payables?

3)　What are your goals for making money? What are your profitability goals? How will you know you are financially successful? How will you know you are making money?

4)　How will you determine what you will be paid for your services or products? How will you handle late payments or customers who fail to pay?

5) Why are your services or products worth your customers paying for them?

Reflect, meditate on and/or pray about all of your responses.

LESSON FOUR

PARTNERS, BOARDERS OR FREELOADERS:
KNOW THE DIFFERENCE

But they all alike began to make excuses.
LUKE 14:18 (NIV)

Many are called but few are chosen.
MATTHEW 22:14

In both versions from Matthew and Luke we are reminded that not everyone who tells you they are committed to your success really will be. There will be all kinds of people who will tell you that they want to see you succeed and they are there to help you. Just remember that when business gets tough, you will hear more excuses than you will hear solutions.

The lesson of accepting the fact that not everyone who joins you in your business endeavor shares your vision and passion has been one of the most difficult lessons to learn in building my business. One of the toughest decisions I had to make in building my business was to part ways with my business partners who had helped develop the concept for the business.

The dissolution of the partnership began early in the development of the business. A conflict surfaced between two of the three partners. One partner felt that another one of the partners had grossly disrespected her during an interaction. When trying to understand what happened between the two of them, I recommended that the four of us meet for dinner.

As I was preparing to go to dinner the passage in Luke in which Jesus shares the parable about a man who invites guests to a great banquet kept pressing in my mind. I stopped to read the passage in its entirety before leaving to meet the others. By the end of the evening, I realized that the passage was God's way of letting me know that the decision I would soon have to make was going to be a tough one.

As it turned out only one of the other three partners came to dinner, the two involved in the conflict did not show up. As I drove home, I contemplated a tough question: if this conflict was going to keep us from communicating, then what other more serious challenges would drive us apart?

September 11, 2001 hit and, of course, turned the economic outlook upside down for any thoughts of progressive business development. Certainly the fledgling Galilee Agency in its infancy was hit hard - money invested was drying up and the prospect of new clients was dismal. I sat in my office at home many days and nights wondering how the business was going to survive and, more importantly, how I was going to survive. With a son in college, a mortgage and other bills, as well as a dedicated assistant trying to hang in there with me until cash was flowing, I found that none of the partners called to check on me. It became apparent that I was the only partner making the emotional and financial investment required to survive during tough times. The other partners were still working full-time and had limited time to invest in building the business.

My accountant advised me to think of buying each partner out for $1.00 since the business had very little value. From a business perspective, this made sense, however, from an emotional perspective this was a tough decision that I dreaded having to make. I called a board meeting of the partners to discuss the current reality of "our" business and again only one of the three partners came to the meeting. This was the same partner who had come to dinner that previous night. These were my friends and yet it became apparent that although we wanted to build a business, we did not all have the same vision, passion or commitment that the business needed to weather difficult times. So after much prayer and deliberation I made the tough decision and sent each partner a letter asking for their support to buy them out. They all agreed reluctantly to sign the agreement. We have continued to keep in touch for the past nine years, however, our relationship has never been the same.

The partnership experience taught me a valuable lesson about ensuring that bylaws are in place to help address those tough decisions that surely will arise during tough times. In the past ten years I have had several opportunities to partner with other individuals both formally and informally. As a result of the lesson learned about shared vision and partnerships, I now know what questions to ask to determine if the partnership is viable and beneficial.

I have found that when you experience any level of success, you will find many who will want to be a part of your success. Those who will want to join you will come in different forms. You will need to know the differences. There will be those individuals who will want to work with you and then those who will want to learn from you. And, of course, there will be those who will just want to take from you. I have divided the joiners into two major categories: boarders and freeloaders. It will be important for you to know the difference.

Boarders can sometimes bring a competency that you need for your business. Unfortunately some boarders will only want to join you in order to build their own businesses. The key here is to ensure that you have a formal agreement as you would with any "boarder or renter." You will need to outline what services and products you expect and what are you willing to give in return.

I have had many "boarders" in the past nine years. Most of them indicated that they wanted to help me, and others indicated they wanted to learn from me. As with any boarding arrangement there are the boarders that make your situation better and then there are those that make it worse.

Perhaps one of my most memorable boarders is an individual who struggled to accept directions from me. He indicated he wanted to learn and yet challenged every idea I presented. Any project I assigned him took additional time to complete because he would never follow the directions I outlined. It became apparent that he did not want to follow the agreement outlined for him. At one point the client and other associates working with me on the project acknowledged that he was not to be trusted. Although the agreement I had with him indicated that he was not to solicit business from the client, he attempted to do this without my knowledge. The client notified me immediately. I sent a letter to him reiterating our signed agreement. I have not worked with him again.

"Freeloaders" can be hard to discern because they often begin by offering their services "free." They will want to learn from you or help you because you are a friend, or family member. Be careful and mindful of the freeloader

- they will drain your time, energy, resources and even your business. As I always tell my sons: there is nothing free in America, especially in business.

Perhaps the best freeloader was one who wanted to work with me so that we both could increase our business opportunities. She was going to leverage her expertise to help us secure opportunities and I was going to do the same. She was very good with her approach. It started with coffee, then dinner, inspirational emails and even gifts. The problem became obvious when I leveraged my relationships to secure business opportunities for her. To date, she has not returned the favor. I learned that this individual wanted to take advantage of my relationships and have free access to the knowledge and experience I have worked hard to acquire.

It is still important to emphasize that there might be opportunities to form partnerships or develop strategic alliances in order to successfully fulfill your mission or deliver your services. I started a successful strategic alliance with an individual, and we are "boarders" for each other on different occasions. This individual and I had spent several years working together, getting to know each other, and, more importantly, learning that we had a shared vision.

Knowing the character or spirit of the individuals that you are going to work with is as important as knowing what you want to achieve. Here's where knowing who you are and what your purpose is becomes extremely critical. It will be difficult to know who you can effectively work or partner with if you do not know what you stand for, or what the mission/purpose is for you and for your business.

LESSON FOUR WORKSHEET
Partners, Boarders or Freeloaders: Know The Difference

1)   Are you clear on the vision you have for your business? In the book of Habakkuk 2:1 in the Bible, we are encouraged to write down our vision and make it plain. Is your vision written and shared by everyone who works with you?

2)   If you have partners, or need partners, what bylaws govern your business decisions regarding their role in, or relationship to, your business?

3) How will you determine if you need partners, or others, to help you with your business?

4) What key characteristics or qualifications do potential partners, or others working with you, need to have?

5) What services/products can others help you to produce and/or deliver?

Reflect, meditate on and/or pray about all of your responses.

LESSON FIVE

NOT ALL BUSINESS IS GOOD BUSINESS: KNOW YOUR "FISH"

Put out into the deep water and let down the nets for a catch ... and when they had done so, they caught such a large number of fish that their nets began to break.

LUKE 5:4,6 (NIV)

In the above passage Luke tells of fisherman who had been fishing all night and had not caught any fish. They were very discouraged and Jesus told them to put their nets out again, and with some trepidation they complied. Immediately their nets began to fill with fish. The fishermen called nearby fishermen to come help them gather the catch, however, after awhile their nets broke from the fill and their ship began to sink.

Most people have read and understood this passage as a testament of how Jesus' blessings are bountiful. However, it is important to understand that with blessings come boundaries. The lesson learned here in building a business is that not all fish need to be caught and some fish can sink your boat. Not all business is good business.

There is a saying that any business is good business. As a result of another difficult lesson I learned, I can say with certainty that not all business is good business. You need to know your fish before you catch them. This lesson came in 2003 when I was asked by one of my former business partners to help a prominent organization coordinate their annual membership meeting. The first sign of a problem came early in the process. What became apparent quickly was that this type of work was outside my mission and scope of services. However, I needed revenue - I had been fishing "all night," that is, for a very long time, and had caught very little fish.

After meeting with the key leaders of the regional organization, I submitted my proposal to help them identify key speakers, develop a marketing campaign and coordinate inviting the 2004 presidential candidates to participate in a forum on behalf of the membership. Because this was outside my scope of service I had no idea exactly what I was proposing to provide for the organization. It soon became apparent that they also had no idea of what they wanted or needed.

When the presidential candidate forum progressed to become a national event requiring intervention from the FBI, the State Department, and the U.S. Department of Homeland Security, it was obvious that I had caught more fish than my net could hold. Satellite trucks from all the major news outlets as well as other media began to converge on Charlotte. The Mayor at the time, as well as the local Chief of Police, called my office in flurries trying to understand what was going on in "their city."

The organization's national leaders called an emergency meeting with the regional leadership demanding answers as to how could something like this happen without their approval. At the same time the meeting was being held, I received a frantic call that half of the candidates scheduled for the forum were stuck in Arizona. Apparently, there was a problem with their plane from Phoenix. The candidates had all been in Arizona the night before for a major nationally televised debate between the democratic candidates. The earliest the stranded candidates were expected to arrive in Charlotte was eight o'clock, exactly one hour after the broadcast was scheduled to end. To further complicate matters, the candidates who had arrived earlier were demanding additional tickets and seats for their supporters. Needless to say, I had more fish than my net could handle.

There was much more that happened in the course of this story, however, the lesson here is that by the end of this project, I was physically, emotionally, intellectually, spiritually and financially broke. My net had broken and my boat was sinking.

When I approached the organization afterwards seeking additional compensation for miraculously producing more than what I had proposed, they refused to pay more. After much pressure the organization finally relented and sent what they felt was warranted. The payment was significantly less than what I had earned. Because I had spent the past four months putting this organization front and center in the national news, I had not spent time developing any other business or potential clients. When I came out of this experience, it was painfully clear that not all business is good business. This business did not align with my mission/purpose.

This became a major turning point in the development of my business. After that mournful and weepy afternoon in my kitchen in November, my purpose became clear and what I was supposed to "be" also became very clear. I began to develop clarity regarding my calling, or what I was supposed to be doing. At the end of 2003, my net had been broken. It took another year before I fully discovered, understood and embraced my purpose for my business.

In January 2004, I began to learn to walk in my purpose. It was only when I could not see what I expected to see that I began to understand that the same voice that had called me to start my business was now speaking to me about my purpose. I was obviously not experiencing fulfillment on any level in my life. I had to learn to walk by faith and yet my faith needed an anchor.

What I discovered is that our purpose is like a hub of a wheel, like that of a car tire, providing stability and the center anchoring the tire to the vehicle. It does not matter what surface the tire treads upon, as long as the hub connects the tire to the car, the car is able to move. Purpose for our lives and our organizations works the same way - it does not matter what we experience, the hub, or our purpose, is what holds us on the road.

At the beginning of 2004, I was limping out of a potential financial nightmare - I may have had less than $50 in my bank accounts, personal and business. I had no clients and no prospect of clients. As I stood in line in the post office one day, I had a very strong inclination to get my passport in order. I laughed out loud since I knew I had no money to buy bus fare, not to mention airfare. When I approached the counter for some reason I asked for a passport application anyway.

When I returned home that day I had a message from a client in South Carolina wanting me to take on a large project. This had been my very first client when I started the business in 2001. I still have a copy of their check on the wall in my office.

Over the next couple of months I worked hard to prepare and develop the large project. While working on the project, one of my business associates and now close friend, Josephine Washington, called to see if I could go to Spain to represent her on a project. Of course, I remembered I had put the passport application away in the excitement of returning the call to the client in South Carolina, and so I was not available to go to Spain at the time.

Another request came for me to go to Venezuela to be a part of two business associates' wedding. Although I did not go to Venezuela, I did complete the passport application and meanwhile other projects and clients started to come along. The work all related to aligning my mission with my vision. As I prepared for each project I discovered more about my role and purpose in this work. I learned that I could not teach what I had not learned.

So what appeared to be unimaginable early on in 2004, came to be. On November 30, 2004, I landed in Geneva, Switzerland to begin my work as "spiritual advisor." I had been asked to be a member of a leadership development team working with an international organization. As coaches, our work was to align the leaders with the organization's mission, vision and values. We were asked to align the culture, character or spirit of the leaders with that of the organization. For the next two years our work not only took us to Switzerland, it also took us to France, Hungary, Germany, Vienna and to Spain, twice.

It was only when I understood my purpose, that my business began to get traction and to follow new paths. Not all business is good business or the fish that you want in your net. However, once you understand the purpose of your business, fishing gets easier and you will know the type of work that your business needs in order for it to grow. When you understand your purpose, you will understand how much weight your business can bear. In other words, you will understand your boundaries and how to avoid breaking your nets.

It is important to know your business, your purpose, your mission or your destiny. By understanding these key principles you will know the business you want, for not all business is good business. Once you understand your purpose and the purpose of your business, you will be able to determine which fish is best for your business. Just because a fish is big does not mean that it is the best fish. Some of the best fish will come from places you can not see, they may be very deep in the water. Fishing for this business may require that you go deep sea fishing. It takes much more effort to fish in deep waters than it takes to fish in shallow water. Some fish may even get away before you are successful in landing them in your boat.

Just remember that if you spend all of your resources fishing in one place for too long, you may miss the possibility of catching other fish. You will need to know how much weight your line, net and/or boat can bear. For if either breaks, you can lose business and potentially you may lose your business. For certain, you will find that you are not aligned with your purpose.

LESSON FIVE WORKSHEET
Not All Business Is Good Business - Know Your "Fish"

1)   Do you understand how your services or products relate to your mission/purpose?

2)   Have you assessed your client or customer profile? Do you have any one customer or client that generates more than 40% of your current revenue?

3)   How will you handle customer or client requests that fall outside your scope of services or product offering?

4) What actions will you take to ensure that you only "fish" for the business you want/need?

5) Develop a list of "fish" you need to catch for your business. Ensure that your list is made up of those clients, customers and/or resources that you need to grow your business.

Reflect, meditate on and/or pray about all of your responses.

LESSON SIX

MAKE SURE YOUR "NET" IS WORKING

Throw your net on the "right" side of the boat and you will find some.

JOHN 21:6 (NIV)

This passage is John's version of the fishermen catching more fish than they could have imagined possible to catch. John's version of the fishing miracle supports the lesson I have learned about ensuring that your nets are in the "right" place to catch the fish that you do want and need. In other words, it is important to network with a purpose - cast your nets in places where you know you will find the right fish, or the right business.

This lesson took a few years to learn and has been a lesson critical to my ability to find the business I needed, and the fish I really wanted. Early on in building my business, I attended a lot of networking events, some just to be with other people. Early in the development of my business, I did not receive many invitations from friends for lunch or other social activities. I attended networking activities out of necessity, for a good meal, an occasional glass of wine, or just to have a conversation with another human.

I joined organizations whose missions say that they are about networking with the hope that I would develop some relationships for potential business. Through one of these organizations I learned that unless you network with a purpose of building your business, you will spend a lot of time and money to only end up with empty nets.

I joined an organization as a result of an invitation from one of the organization's more prominent members. She had indicated that the organization needed more diversity and felt I could bring a lot of value to achieving this objective. I attended several lunches and dinners and was soon asked to serve on one of the annual program committees. The committee met several times during the year at different members' places of business.

After I left each committee meeting I always felt that I had gone fishing without my net. The committee members all had very successful businesses and saw the meetings as opportunities to share their successes with the other members. I was a struggling entrepreneur and the time I was giving to these meetings appeared to have been consumed by the members need to socialize. Even organizational meetings dedicated to networking did little to promote doing business with other members - they were primarily set up for socializing.

During one of the meetings I was given an opportunity to showcase my business by setting up a display to feature my services. Other than the few guests that I had invited, none of the members visited my display or even stopped by to ask questions about my business.

By the end of my tenure on the program committee I knew that I was in not in the right place for casting my net or for networking. When deciding not to renew my membership I was honest with the member who had invited me to join the organization. To this day I respect that she admitted to me that the main reason she had joined the organization was for socializing.

I have found other organizations who proclaim to promote networking or business relationship development yet often their major focus is to promote socializing more than networking. This is why it is important that you understand the objective of networking.

The word network means an "interrelated chain, group or system" (Merriam-Webster Dictionary). The key word here is "interrelated." To reinforce the business translation, if networking is to occur, then there needs to be a relationship or an interrelated connection with what your business needs are at the time.

You will need to be intentional and target your networking. For example, if you need some help with technology then you need to network with groups that have individuals whose primary focus is technology. Be clear about what you need or want during your time at a targeted network event. With the proliferation of social media networking mediums such as LinkedIn, Facebook and Twitter you may also find it easier to articulate your needs or services online.

I suggest however that you will still need to rely on your keen sense of networking whether you begin the process online or in person. You will need to get comfortable with meeting people in order to discuss your needs and to develop relationships with individuals who may have information to help you target your networking or to ensure that you have the "right" net in the "right" place!

As we saw in Lesson Four, you will also need to know when to end those network relationships where the connection is "cold," or there is no connection. You will meet a lot of people who will make promises to connect you to individuals who can help you. You will need to quickly identify those individuals that tend to be more talk than action. If not, you will spend a lot of your valuable time making calls and following up with these "cold" individuals only to be disappointed.

I get a kick out of those individuals who always insist that you get with them to have lunch or coffee and there is no follow through regardless of your efforts to make it happen. Every time you see them, it is the same line: "let's do lunch or coffee." One individual I know will even go to the trouble of scheduling a lunch time. Invariably, however, at the last minute he always forgets the appointment or has something that comes up. Now when he offers for us to do lunch, I just smile. I am not sure what it is about these individuals other than perhaps it is good for their egos.

You will know when you have a "hot" connection when networking. The other person works as hard as you to make the next step happen. I learned this lesson after spending almost a year attending several events sponsored by networking groups. Most of which were only designed for social networking rather than connecting businesses.

The exception to this was a breakfast group I was invited to join by another entrepreneur. This entrepreneur had just started a private physical therapy business. It was also very clear that she knew her business was aligned with her purpose. She provides physical therapy and massages for women who are either undergoing treatment for cancer or have had a partial or full mastectomy. I met her at a friend's home during a Pamper Party. She was giving massages for those attending the party.

During my massage she felt the tension in my body. She asked what type of work I was doing. I told her that I had my own business. She responded,

"I am also doing what I know I have been called to do in my life."

As I shared, some of the challenges I was experiencing, she told me about this networking group that she felt was unlike others she had attended. She promised to call me and invite me to the next meeting. Keeping her promise, she called me two weeks later and invited me to the next meeting. She also noted that she had a potential client that she wanted me to meet. At the meeting I met Reuben Benson, Agent/Owner with Nationwide Insurance.

As a owner of Benson & Associates, Reuben wanted to develop a strategy to increase efficiencies in his office while also increasing his market share. It was the end of 2001 and business was almost non-existent for me. Reuben and I set up an appointment to meet a week later. He immediately decided that he wanted me to help him with developing solutions to get the results he needed. Amazingly, he requested a proposal that outlined work for the next twelve months.

The lesson here is it did not take multiple networking meetings before I was introduced to Reuben, and working with him and Nationwide Insurance. The net actually worked in this situation. As fate would have it, five years later when I moved into our current location I needed property insurance for the office. I contacted Marlon Nesbeth, my life and health insurance broker to ask her to help me get the property insurance. Marlon called one afternoon to verify the office location. When I gave her the address and location, she responded excitedly, "What a small world!"

Marlon noted that she had just left the office of Reuben Benson whose office was located in the same building that I was planning to move my organization into. One of the recommendations I had given Reuben when I worked with him five years earlier was to reduce his office space for more efficient operations. He had taken my advice and moved his office to a new location. Seven years later not only are we in the same building, The Galilee Agency is now right next door to Reuben's Nationwide office.

The moral of this story goes back to understanding and knowing when you are in purpose. When you are in purpose things tend to align and you will know that your "net" is working!

I can not promise you that every contact you make at a networking event or activity is going to result in a contract or an outcome like the one

I had with Reuben and Nationwide Insurance. I can, however, tell you that if your net is not working you will spend a lot of time meeting people and not building key business relationships. If you are attending or participating in networking events and/or activities and you or your business have not benefited, then your net is not working.

LESSON SIX WORKSHEET
Make Sure Your "Net" Is Working

What organizations or social networks do you belong to, or need to join, to help you develop key relationships for your business?

1) List five things you need for your business that networking will help you obtain.

(a)

(b)

(c)

(d)

(e)

2) List five individuals you need to meet who can help you with your business.

(a)

(b)

(c)

(d)

(e)

3) List five individuals you already know that can help you meet individuals that can help you with your business.

(a)

(b)

(c)

(d)

(e)

4) Write the networking statement that you will use at your next networking event, or online, to describe the relationships you need to develop to help your business.

Reflect, meditate on and/or pray about all of your responses.

LESSON SEVEN

PEOPLE DO BUSINESS WITH PEOPLE THEY KNOW

From everyone who has been given much, much will be demanded;
and from the one who has been entrusted with much, much more
will be asked.

LUKE 12:48 (NIV)

Another major lesson I have learned in building my business is that people do business with people they know, trust and respect. Although you will need to be intentional with your networking you will also need to invest time in building true business relationships.

Perhaps one of the things that I am most proud of regarding The Galilee Agency is that more than 60% of the clients and customers that we currently have cultivated have come as a result of relationships that we have invested in developing.

Two of my current clients are also two of my dearest friends. In addition to being clients, they have been great resources and referral sources. Tana Greene, President of Strataforce, is one of these special clients. Strataforce is a light industrial staffing company located in Davidson, North Carolina. Tana was speaking in Chicago and noted in her speech that she had a consultant and coach helping her to grow her business while also helping her develop as a business leader. Michelle Benjamin, President of Benjamin Enterprises, a national facility support staff augmentation company based out of New York, immediately approached Tana after her speech and asked for my contact information. Before Tana could let me know to expect her call, Michelle had already called and the rest has been a phenomenal experience.

In addition to these two special clients' relationships, I have learned that building relationships with those you can help can also help you. This is referred to as building social capital.

In 2001, I had the opportunity to meet an individual at an event that we both had been asked to attend at the last minute. After exchanging pleasantries, we recognized that each of our businesses could benefit from the other's one core competency. Born in Venezuela, Astrid Chirinos had come to the United States with her parents as a child. After completing her education and pursuing a career in the marketing and design industry, she spent a short stint with a major financial organization. Realizing that her free spirit needed a bigger arena than corporate America could provide, Astrid had also decided to start her own business in 2001. Although our initial meeting was unplanned, our ability to find purpose in working together surfaced instantaneously.

The one thing that I have learned from our unique relationship is the importance of building social capital. As an immigrant with English as her second language, Astrid has learned to develop those skills that would help her bridge the gaps and connect with individuals and organizations critical to fulfilling her mission and objectives. She has taught me the value of identifying those organizations whose missions align with mine and that can afford me an opportunity to make a difference beyond my business.

As my business began to grow, I have been asked to join community organizations, and to serve on boards of several organizations. During the interview process for these opportunities I have learned how to determine if what is being represented is actually being done in the organizations. I have learned to take my commitment to serve on these boards as part of my purpose for who I am and what I am supposed to be doing. Other board members often share that "one can always count on Brenda to ask the right questions or to say what needs to be said."

My belief is that if I am going to invest my time and resources in an organization, then it is important that I add value. As a result of following this principle, I have been able to develop relationships that have led to subsequent business relationships for me. This happened with a client who I had the opportunity to work with on a special advisory council. The client noted that he was impressed with my integrity and wanted to ensure that I was included in a bid process for a major project with his organization. We subsequently were awarded the contract and continue to work with this client today.

In most of the organizations that I have been involved with in the past five years, I have also had the honor to take on a leadership role. More importantly, I have developed relationships built from respect and trust with other individuals in these organizations. These relationships have led to other relationships which have led to opportunities for me to fulfill my mission while growing my business. In other words, we have made social investments to build relationships and social capital. One such relationship is the work I have been involved in with one of our local PBS stations, WTVI. As a facilitator for community conversations on "Love and Forgiveness," I have even had the opportunity to go to Kalamazoo and back. Through this process I have had the opportunity to participate in one of the most meaningful personal and professional growth experiences in my life.

Building true business relationships will mean that you will need to invest your time in work for which you may not receive immediate financial compensation. It will, however, help you to develop social capital, a requirement and investment for those entrusted to do much.

LESSON SEVEN WORKSHEET
People Do Business With People They Know

1)   What is the mission of the organizations you belong to? How do these missions align with the mission for your business?

2)   What committees are you serving on in these organizations? How can your work on these committees help you achieve your mission?

3) What actions have you taken to ensure that you are developing relationships with others in these organizations?

4) What work/services have you provided for these organizations that you did not receive compensation for, or for which you offered a significant discount?

5) How can what you do/provide help your community, or make a difference in someone else's life?

Reflect, meditate on and/or pray about all of your responses.

LESSON EIGHT

DO THE LITTLE THINGS RIGHT
TO MAKE THE BIG THINGS HAPPEN

But each of you must be careful how you build ...
... and the quality of each man's work will be seen.

I CORINTHIANS 3:10,13

Paul's letter to the church in Corinth was to remind the church of the importance of taking time to do things right the first time. This age-old quality principle is critical to any successful business. Paul's words were a reminder to the people that there are no shortcuts to doing good work - in the end, it is about the doing the little things right that will ensure that good things and big things happen!

As we struggle today with the economic crises of the world's financial markets, CEOs of failing organizations along with executives of other struggling organizations are being called into question about their leadership and the actions taken by their respective organizations. After the financial crisis of 2008, many of us were asking how can certain decisions be made with other people's money and/or livelihoods. Why were bonuses being paid to some while thousands were being given "pink slips," and losing their businesses and homes? Regardless of whether you have a multi-billion dollar organization or you are an emerging entrepreneur, Paul's admonition to the church of Corinth is relevant today - the quality of each man's work will eventually be seen!

This lesson is one that can be difficult to honor, especially when you are working hard to build your business, keep food on the table and/or a roof over your head. However, building your business with a commitment to excellence and core values of accountability, execution, integrity and respect will ensure that you will always be proud of your work and your business.

Perhaps the two most challenging aspects of any business include keeping good records and evaluating your results. Early on in my business, my accountant encouraged me to use Quick Books to help me track my financial transactions. I taught myself the rudimentary fundamentals of the program and, for the most part, did well keeping records using the software early on with my business. On the other hand, I made little to no money at that time so tracking the business was pretty simple. As my business began to grow, keeping records became more and more difficult - monthly input became quarterly input. Eventually, I found myself scrambling to organize records from the past year in order for my accountant to make some sense out of what I had accomplished.

By 2006, the business had begun to take off and I had several major projects, and several consultants and contractors working with The Galilee Agency. This meant not only keeping track of records for the company but also ensuring that we had proper documentation of tax records for 1099 contractors and others. By the time I understood what needed to happen for 2006, we were in the middle of 2007. Although we were able to meet the deadlines to get documentation out to the contractors, we still had other liabilities that needed to be addressed.

These liabilities began to adversely impact The Galilee Agency's profitability and capacity to grow. I began to look for financial assistance to help liquidate some of the liability. As a result of the difficulty in the early years, I was not going to qualify for credit assistance from any financial institution. In fact, one young eager small business financial consultant from a now failed financial institution recommended that I go through credit counseling with the local Family Service organization. She recommended that I take some classes on how to build credit. When I met with the Family Services Counselor, he was embarrassed after reading my business vitae and apologized for wasting my time. It was not that I didn't know what to do - I just hadn't done what needed to be done.

After working to develop a business case, I was referred to an investor. The investor immediately saw value in my business case and agreed to invest in my business over a five-month period. After working out an agreement with my attorney, the investor made two payments. Unfortunately, his business was impacted by the economic downturn in 2008. His misfortune created a traumatic ripple effect and aftershock for my business. I had to let go key employees as a result of the investment debacle. It also meant that I needed to develop a new business strategy.

Although I had a legal agreement with the investor, my integrity and respect for the investor told me that it would serve little purpose to pursue legal action against him. The lesson in this situation: when seeking an investment of capital get what you need in one lump sump payment, or in the shortest time period as possible.

Perhaps when the investor rebounds he will keep his commitment and if not, I will look for other innovative strategies to address any financial challenges. In fact, this situation forced me to go back to my original business plan and the fundamentals of what I wanted to do with my business from the beginning. After reviewing the original plan I remembered a strategy that I wanted to pursue: by year five I had planned to begin teaching and writing about what I have learned on my journey. *From Zero To Faith* is the first book that I knew I needed to write. The purpose-inspired leadership series, "Being the Best!" that we now offer is also part of the strategic plan for me to teach and share what I have learned.

My commitment to excellence, however, remains unwavering. Practicing the fundamentals of the values of accountability and execution, however, continue to challenge me. Taking care of those critical and fundamental records, documenting results require taking time away from the things that energize me. And yet, I have learned that these tasks are critical to building a successful business.

I once had a client whose only record of how his business was going was to look at his bank records. We subsequently worked on developing a financial management system to help him track income, expenses and other liabilities. And yet, as a business consultant I sometimes still struggle with the fundamentals much like the shoemaker who has no shoes.

To sustain a commitment to excellence will require that you practice developing accountability. As an entrepreneur or business owner you ultimately are accountable for the outcomes of your business - the buck starts and stops with you. It is your business and you are accountable for what happens or does not happen, you own it! One of the best practices for developing ownership is planning.

For those who fail to plan … can plan to fail!

Planning may be a little thing to do but without it you will find it very difficult to make big things happen. One of the key services that I provide for my clients is developing strategic "action" plans. The emphasis is on the word "action." Although the plan needs to be strategic and needs to serve as a blueprint for guiding your business toward long-term outcomes or vision, the plan serves very little purpose if no one ever looks to see if it is working. Utilizing a balanced scorecard[4] approach you will need to develop outcomes, goals, measures and milestones that will help you to evaluate if you are executing or achieving the results you want. These objectives will help assess and evaluate aspects of your financial, customer, marketing, and other internal processes, as well as human capital, and perhaps community stewardship. Critical to developing these objectives you will need to ensure that someone in the organization "owns" the results. Often I have clients who will want to have multiple owners for an outcome, this will work if each of the owners have equal ownership. If this is not the case then I recommend one owner for each outcome. Remember, however, as the owner of the business you are ultimately the owner of the vision and the overall plan.

Once a quarter or at least once a year, I recommend bringing all the outcome owners together to evaluate the strategic plan, and the progress and results the organization has made. My clients have found that although they have good intentions to review the plan … they sometimes struggle with the process. In most cases, the primary purpose of their businesses is not about facilitating a strategic planning meeting. This is where The Galilee Agency comes in to help them. Monitoring how you and your business are doing with the plan develops accountability and helps to ensure execution. Since this is often not your primary focus for your business, I recommend you hire an executive coach or mentor who will help you in your role of developing accountability and driving execution.

Again, it does not matter what size business you have, it is important to pay attention to how you build your business. Remember, the quality of your work will be seen. You will need to determine processes for dealing with those elements of your business that may appear to take you away from what

4   Kaplan, Robert S., and David P. Norton. The Balanced Scorecard: Translating Strategy into Action. Boston, Mass: Harvard Business School Press, 1996.

you enjoy doing. I have found that developing a strategic plan, or an annual "main thing" focus plan, can help you with dealing with the fundamentals of your business. In order to avoid dealing with those things that can put your business in jeopardy (take it from someone who knows) you must value the fundamentals of doing the little things right if you want big things to happen.

Another little thing that you will need to pay attention to is very simple: integrity. Integrity is about doing what you say you are going to do. There are so many of us who are willing and proud to declare that we have integrity. However, I am not sure what has happened to the meaning of the word "integrity." It appears that for some reason we all do not have the same understanding of the word.

For me, integrity is adhering unconditionally to a value, whether that value is honesty, service, or reliability. If you say that you are going to do something then it is understood that you are being honest and integrity reflects that you do what you said you are going to do. Unfortunately, however, integrity appears to be one of those little things that people struggle with in business. A lack of integrity can be extremely damaging to your business reputation when people discover that you are not honest. When they discover that you do not have integrity, you and your business are in deep trouble.

An example of this type of trouble is in the story of an individual who asked for my support on a major project. Let's call him Mr. Sponsor. The opportunity was a challenging one in which I was to have responsibility for developing the curriculum for a training program. After spending several days working on the framework for the project, I went to meet with Mr. Sponsor. His secretary mistakenly thought that I was there for another reason and had me wait in a conference room for him. After about fifteen minutes Mr. Sponsor came in accompanied by another gentleman. I could tell by the look on Sponsor's face, that he was shocked to see me in the conference room. He tried to remain composed, introducing me to the gentleman who had accompanied him to the conference room. After a long moment of awkwardness, Mr. Sponsor asked me to step outside.

He told me that apparently there had been some confusion regarding the project. I was informed that the gentleman now in the conference room had been selected to do the work I was supposed to have completed. It took all I had to hold my embarrassment, anger and yes, tears in check. I quickly went back into the conference room to gather my belongings. I was shocked, stunned and in complete disbelief as to what had just transpired. How could this have happened? What happened with this little thing called integrity? It was no where to be found! Mr. Sponsor had decided in the process to bring this other gentleman in to work on the project. Apparently they were old friends and belonged to the same fraternity. I later learned that it was important for this man to work with the client. He needed an entrée into the company and Mr. Sponsor was his ticket. It did not matter at this point how I felt, my time had been wasted and I had been greatly disrespected by Mr. Sponsor.

Once I shared what had happened to me with others, I discovered that others had similar experiences with Mr. Sponsor. We all agreed he lacked integrity. His reputation for not being honest and not having integrity quickly swept through the business community. The one thing about not having integrity: it does not take long for others to know about it! Although I run into him on occasions I have never confronted Mr. Sponsor about what happened that day - I didn't have to, he no longer has the client and, for the most part, is not in business.

That little thing of having integrity is critical, and a big thing for your success in business. It is important that whatever you tell your clients, customers, employees and business associates that you can or will do, you must be able to do it. You are accountable for the outcomes regardless of what happens. If you can not keep your commitments, promises or deliver the level of services/products your customers are expecting it is better to let them know than to have your integrity compromised.

Planning to develop accountability and driving execution are critical little things you will need to do if you want big things to happen for your business. Doing what you promise and what you say is as important as the product/ services you provide. Integrity is what will make your products/services more valuable to your customers. It represents respect for your customers, for your clients, and for you. Remember, the quality of your work will be seen, so do the little things right in order to make the big things happen!

LESSON EIGHT WORKSHEET
Do The Little Things Right To Make The Big Things Happen

1)   What have you defined as your key strategic outcomes for the next two years? How are you measuring your progress toward achieving these outcomes?

2)   Who in your organization is responsible for tracking results and/or keeping records for the organization? What type of reports or records do you keep or have in place to ensure that results are being tracked?

3)   What agreements or contracts do you have that may need legal review? When was the last time you attended a business legal seminar?

4) When was the last financial review completed for your business? Was this with your banker, accountant, CPA or your best friend?

5) Who do you have as a business mentor or coach to help you with difficult business decisions?

6) How will others rate your level of integrity or your ability to keep promises and agreements? Will they say that your actions, services/products are always what you promise?

Reflect, meditate on and/or pray about all of your responses.

LESSON NINE

YOU HAD BETTER "SWEAT" THE DETAILS

... And there are diversities of operations, but it is the same God
which worketh all in all ...

I CORINTHIANS 12:6

As we saw in the previous lesson, it is important that you have a keen sense of ownership in what is happening with your business. It is even more important that you understand that you will need to manage and operate the details of your business. As mundane as this may sound, it is often difficult to achieve.

Again in Corinthians - Chapter 12, Paul is writing to the church of Corinth reminding the followers that although we have the spirit of God dwelling inside of us, we still have different gifts and purposes with which we must align and leverage if we are to prosper more effectively. As we saw in Lesson One, we all have a unique purpose and what we choose to do with our businesses can be greatly enhanced if we operate from a place of purpose.

This was in evidence as my father continued to build his enterprise of selling vegetables, peas and beans and expanded to fresh shucked corn and sugar cane juice. I remember an adventure when my father loaded me and my brothers, Luther and Tommy, onto his old army surplus vegetable truck and took us somewhere down near his birthplace in Uchee Hill, Alabama. I had to be about eight or nine years old. It was a typical hot muggy summer day in Alabama. Uchee Hill is located in Russell County, Alabama. It is about 15 miles from my hometown, Columbus.

The first chore upon our arrival for the day was to clean my father's parents' grave site behind the old home church. Covered with overgrown weeds, my father and brothers had their work cut out. I watched from the back of the truck drinking my favorite Nehi peach soda to keep cool.

Somewhere during the process, one of Tommy's feet became wedged between the headstone of my grandfather, Charlie's old grave site and the overgrowth surrounding the grave. The more Tommy struggled to get free the firmer it appeared his foot became wedged. It was as if the spirit of my grandfather was pulling Tommy's leg into the grave. Tommy began to panic and scream, "He's got me, he's got me!" As he did so, my father, Luther and I had to pull Tommy from the grave. My father tried to keep his composure in front of us. However, it was quite apparent we were all more than a little frightened by the experience. When we got home later, I overheard my father telling my mother that the incident at the grave had shaken him "something terrible."

With Tommy now completely shaken from the grave experience, he was excused from helping with the next chore. That meant my brother Luther had to take on the chore of helping to grind sugar cane. We had picked up the sugar cane along the way to Uchee Hill. The process to grind sugar cane at that time typically required a mule. A harness was placed on the mule. The harness was connected to some type of homemade grinder (we do all this stuff now in our kitchen with our "juicers"). With encouragement from the grinder's owner, the mule moves around in a circle connected to the grinding contraption. As I have shared, my father came from a very enterprising family where the concept of locomotion did not always depend on animals. Since we did not have a mule, my father connected my brother Luther to the harness and with much "encouragement," Luther began the process of grinding the sugar cane into juice. In addition to juice for drinking, my father also made sugar cane syrup from the juice. He sold both of these products as well.

My father knew that in order to deliver the best products for his customers, he had to "sweat" the details. He had to find a way to get the best and freshest products to his customers, and not having a mule only meant he had to find another way to get the best sugar cane juice.

Hopefully in your business you will never have to impersonate being a mule, however, I am certain that you have worked extremely hard or even felt like you had done the work of a mule. In the introduction, I shared a factoid that most entrepreneurs are surprised by how hard they have to work. The adage blood, sweat and tears is more than a phrase when you are a business owner. Shedding blood, sweat and tears can be a common experience for most entrepreneurs. And yet, if you are going to be successful, you better be prepared to do so or else plan to sweat the details.

One of the experiences that helped me understand this lesson came as a result of working on a major project with Astrid Chirinos. We had been retained to develop a major diversity training program for a large international organization. Astrid and I had outlined the timeline for delivery of curriculum, materials and resources. We had pulled together a great team to ensure that we would deliver a superior product. In the middle of the project Astrid and I received a request to meet with another client to present a proposal for services. As the deadline for the original project drew closer, we began to develop the outline for the proposal. As with any major project there will always be challenges with ensuring that all the deliverables are aligned with the key milestones. It can be similar to tricks of concentration such as spinning plates or juggling knives, if one plate or knife falls, the consequences can have devastating impacts. In our situation, we had plates falling and crashing, and knives cutting our jugglers!

The training kits that were scheduled to be ready for the materials had not arrived from the vendor. The printer responsible for their production had a major equipment failure and content that was needed to finish the workbook was lost somewhere between my computer and the graphic artist's computer. We worked around the clock to recover, taking only a few minutes to eat and take bathroom breaks. At one point, the graphic artist fell asleep at his desk - we thought he had fainted because he didn't appear to come around after we shook him to see if he was okay. Everyone's nerves were on edge and tempers flared - team members walked out of the office swearing not to return, only to return after cooling down! As a team, we were determined and committed that we were not going to fail. At another point, when we stopped to review what needed to be done, I reminded the team that we needed each other to achieve this project. As I looked into each of the team members' eyes, all I could see was complete exhaustion.

We all pushed so hard that final night, much like my brother pushing that grinder in Uchee Hill. And then it hit me: we had to prepare the proposal for the other client! The meeting was scheduled for 10 am the next morning and it was 11 pm. It was too late to call and cancel the meeting, a meeting that *we* had requested. All of the key stakeholders would be at the meeting including the president of the organization. As some of our project team members worked to box up the materials for the Federal Express pick up the next morning, Astrid and I turned our attention to the proposal. The training materials had to be in Texas the following day. We were scheduled to fly to Texas later the same day.

As the materials were being boxed up we began to work on the proposal. This was not just any proposal, it included a PowerPoint presentation along with an orientation of the training we were proposing to provide. With less than 12 hours left to develop the proposal, we turned our focus to the new project. I heard the radio announcer in the background tell all of us midnight to dawn workers that "… you are halfway there, … midnighters!" It must have been 3 am! Since I wrote most proposals at that time, I just kept working. The next indication of time came when the team members who had boxed the materials for shipping the night before returned to the office bearing coffee and bagels. At some point during the night they must have left - I can't tell you to this day if they did or not, they only laugh whenever I ask about that night.

At 8:30 am Astrid and I made the last copy of the proposal and presentation. We had to drive across town for the 10 am meeting so there was no time to go home and shower. Fortunately, we kept some toiletries in the office because they definitely were needed at that point. After doing some basic freshening, off we went to present the proposal. When we arrived, we were notified that the meeting was actually scheduled for an hour later. Now our objective was to stay awake long enough in order to make the presentation. We walked and talked to keep ourselves awake. It was becoming increasingly difficult to drink anymore coffee - I was beginning to feel my heart beating irregularly and the ringing in my ears was getting louder. So I finally just found a place to sit down.

While sitting and waiting for the meeting I decided to review the proposal. A cold feeling came over me, there were misspelled words and incomplete sentences throughout the proposal. The presentation had information from other presentations we had presented to other clients. Needless to say, it was embarrassing and not representative of what we wanted to present that day. As we looked at ourselves in the restroom mirror, we realized that we looked as bad as our presentation. Fortunately, the president of the organization had been called to another meeting. We decided not to show the PowerPoint but to turn the meeting into an assessment of the client's needs. This worked to our advantage that day, however, it taught us a valuable lesson: you better make time to sweat the details. If you do not have the time, resources or capacity to put the effort into the details then you can expect that you will not get the outcomes you want.

In Lesson One, we saw the ChangeGrid. The ChangeGrid is a tool to assess your level of readiness in accomplishing a desired outcome or task. If there are some details you need to manage more effectively, the ChangeGrid can help you determine what you may need to do to address this challenge. The principle of the ChangeGrid is based on the concept of tension. No matter what your situation may be, for you to get the results you need you will have to evaluate your current situation.

There are some basic questions you may want to ask yourself in evaluating your situation:

- Am I safe or will I be safe?
- Do I feel secure or will I be more secure if I change?
- Am I happy or will changing make me happy?
- Am I healthy or will I be healthier if I change?

Your responses to these questions will determine the amount of tension you have regarding your situation. Tension is the level of physical, emotional and intellectual activity a person is experiencing at any given moment of time. People pay attention to where there is tension. In the absence of tension there is no productivity. Your success in achieving the change you want is based on your natural or learned ability to monitor and manage tension.

Unfortunately, many of us have spent most of our lives living from a place of fear. As a result we tend to manage our lives and the details of our businesses by reacting and/or working to avoid mistakes. So our ability to manage the tension required to make the necessary changes in our lives or businesses is typically influenced by fear. Taking a look back at the ChangeGrid in Lesson One, you will see that if fear becomes your primary influencer then, in most cases, you will be in a tension state of stress. You will tend to be reactive, feel out of control, and often make decisions that are counterproductive. The example of Astrid and I rushing to get a presentation together that resulted in embarrassment for us and our work is what happens when you operate from a place of stress. Your actions will be ruled by emotions and not logic.

The ChangeGrid helps you to determine what your response state is regarding any particular outcome you want or need. Your responses can range from stress to apathy. If you have reached a level of apathy in your journey as an entrepreneur or business owner, then it may be time to rethink what you are doing and if you are indeed aligned with your purpose. The ideal responses on the ChangeGrid for achieving the outcomes you want will fall somewhere in the range of "power" or "power + stress." When you feel empowered, your ability to effectively evaluate and to consider your options will be optimized. However, if you are looking to change you will need to have a level of tension that creates stress and power. In this state you will most often recognize the need to change, know what you must do and the probability of you deciding to do what needs to be done is very high. Your focus will be on going and not on leaving.

When I think about my father, my brothers and the mule at the sugar cane grinder that summer day, I realized that my father knew that if he wanted to get the best product he would need additional resources and capacity. He knew that in order to get the details that he wanted, he had to be enterprising in how he leveraged his resources. He did not have the mule, yet he knew he had the resources and capacity to get the job done well. My father understood the concept of "sweating" the details.

To develop your personal ChangeGrid for your responses in Lesson One, you may want to visit our website at http://www.galileeagency.com and follow the ChangeGrid link. For a nominal fee, we will send you your personal ChangeGrid and report. We will provide you with feedback regarding your current state of tension as a business owner or entrepreneur. Based on your feedback, each of the outcomes listed in Lesson One can be further analyzed by looking at specific tasks or details that you may need to manage in order to achieve your desired results.

Why is the ChangeGrid important? It will help you to manage the tension required to produce the results you want. It is a critical assessment to help you determine which details you need to pay closer attention to in your business. In other words, what are those details you need to "sweat" in order to achieve what you need/want?

In Lesson Eight, we saw the importance of focusing on the little things to make big things happen. Focusing on the details is equally important, or perhaps more important, in growing your business. It is critical for you to manage details such as proposals, presentations and invoices. It is important that these documents reflect the agreements you have with your clients, customers and suppliers. Invoices you submit to your clients will need to reflect the understanding of the agreement(s) you have with them. This is especially important when your small, developing business is working with large organizations or corporations that process thousands of invoices in a month.

In most cases, the individuals that accept or approve your proposal, or proposed statements of work, know as much about the organization's accounts payable process as they do about the flight path of a butterfly when it first emerges from the cocoon. I prefer not to remember how many times I have been desperately waiting on a promised payment to only find out that the invoice had not been processed or had been misplaced. (By the way, invoices are never misplaced or lost - they just happen to be in 'that stack'.) Sometimes a signature is missing, or the W-9 doesn't match your vendor address, or the invoice needs to be processed in another office in another state (which means there are additional forms that must be completed).

The message here is to ask your business contact for a name in the accounting department. Follow up with this person and ask them to walk you through the organization's required accounts payable process. You may need to learn to work through the details while under duress or contract with someone to manage this process for your business. There are individuals whose primary business model is to sweat the small stuff (details) for small businesses.

The other major detail that you will need to manage is to understand the importance of getting tax identification information and verifying this information upfront before you begin paying contractors or employees. With employees this is typically easy if you understand that individuals can not work in the United States without proper identification indicating that they are eligible to work in the United States. Although the eligibility to work process is straightforward regarding identification, it does not matter how many employees you have working for you, it is important that you complete the I-9 employee eligibility process. There are several laws too in-depth for me to address that regulate this process, however, before hiring anyone (even your mother) please familiarize yourself with this process.

If you work only with individuals who are considered 1099 (subcontractor or contractor) status, it is important that you get and verify their tax identification information before you make any payments to these individuals. The Internal Revenue Services will identify any tax identification information that does not match or is missing from your annual summary (1096) information. Failing to get this information and to verify it can result in potential penalties for your business.

As we saw in Lesson Four, I had to terminate my agreement with a contractor because he was violating the cardinal rule of consultants: *thou shall not steal or covet another consultant's clients* - particularly since he was working for the other consultant (me)! Of course, this was the one contractor whose tax identification information did not match the IRS report. Nothing is harder than to trying to get information from someone you have had to terminate. Ensure you have a good tax accountant on your team or an employee to help you avoid overlooking the detail of getting the proper tax information for your business and for your employees/contractors.

A critical detail that you will need to "sweat" is ensuring that you have the right people doing the right things at the right time in the right place. This continues to be a difficult challenge that business owners and entrepreneurs often face, namely, selecting and hiring the right person for the job.

What makes this challenge even more daunting is when you hire relatives. Just like borrowing money from family, hiring family members can also be a very dicey proposition. What happens when their performance does not meet expectations? What happens when you know you need to let them go? Before you decide to hire a relative or close friend, I recommend you follow the same process you would follow if they were not a relative or friend. I have worked with clients when this did not happen.

Performance expectations need to be outlined for your relatives, or friends, just as you would outline them for other employees, and you do need to pay attention to this detail. If not, I promise you will find that you are sweating more than the details. Once the expectations are outlined, the hardest part (when the real sweating begins) comes when you have to hold family and friends accountable.

When hiring any employees, do your pre-employment verifications thoroughly. If you are having problems getting references to call you back, consider that as a potential red flag. Good references want to help individuals with their employment process. I once had a reference call me from his hospital bed because he wanted to ensure that he provided feedback for a candidate!

Although you may need to hire someone right away, take the time to sweat the details and do your due diligence. If you know you are not a good interviewer, get someone to help you with this part of the process. Quick hiring decisions will typically reveal, sooner or later, that some details have not been addressed. It is interesting, however, to see how long it sometimes takes an entrepreneur/business owner to terminate an employee who obviously is not the right person, doing the right things at the right time in the right place. Hiring the right people for your business and holding them accountable is a detail you must sweat.

Other less serious details, yet important ones, include managing your communications with your clients or potential clients. Sweating this detail includes managing your voicemail and email accounts. Ensure that you have enough capacity for your telephone, as well as cell phone, to avoid having a voicemail box that is "too full" to receive calls. Also, ensure that your voicemail message(s) are current. It tells your client that you do not pay attention to details if your voicemail messages indicate that you are out of the office until Monday and that was two weeks ago. Invest in a cell or PDA that affords you access to your email while you are away from your office. Just keep in mind not to check or respond to emails during the time you are working with or focusing on your clients' needs.

One of the five factors customers indicate as important to them includes responsiveness[5]. You may have the best product, knowledge or service,

5   Parasuraman, A., Valarie A. Zeithaml, and Leonard L. Berry. Servqual, a Multiple-Item Scale for Measuring Customer Perceptions of Service Quality. Cambridge, Mass: Marketing Science Institute, 1986.

however, if your customers or clients can not get in touch with you or you can not respond to their needs in a timely manner, you are in a position to lose customers. Most customers often walk away without telling you why they decided to go with your competition.

Other details to remember include your reliability. Assure your customers that they have made the right decision to do business with you and demonstrate your empathy and ability to understand your customers needs, challenges and environment. The more details you learn about your customers, the more effective you will be in meeting their needs. Find and read articles and other pertinent sources of information about what is happening with your customers and their respective industries. The more customers believe you care about their success, the more they will care about your success. Talk with employees when you visit your customers, as well as when they visit with you. Take the time to learn more about your customers, their concerns and needs.

To appreciate these details, you will need to understand your unique gifts and talents. If your gifts tend to make you a great starter than an implementer or detail manager, then you may need some help in focusing on details that need to be managed. If you are uncomfortable with some details, or do not understand some details for business management, then it will be important that you have someone on your team who is comfortable with these types of details. You may even decide to partner with others who can help you with these details. The lesson here may be that the blessing or unique value proposition your business provides is often experienced in the diversity of the details. Ensure that you understand these details and how important they are to growing your business. I have had to learn painfully that when you fail to value the details, you can plan for the details to cause you to fail.

If you are aligned with your purpose, you will find the necessary resources to help you manage the details of your business. As I have developed my business and aligned with my purpose, I have been able to bring individuals to my team who enjoy managing details more than I do. Cortney Donelson, Program Coordinator for Galilee Agency, is one such person. Cortney has the unique gift to take clients' notes from me and other consultants and work with the details - turning a puzzle into a masterpiece.

I am always amazed at her ability to take stacks of notes and put them into a well-structured executive summary or report. She can do this faster than anyone I've ever met. However, as a result of her speed she sometimes has to focus on improving her accuracy in attending to the details. And because I am a stickler for the details, Cortney and others that work with me have learned that before sending information to me, it needs to pass the Brenda "eye test" for an assessment of the details.

Another detail that I have found critical to business owners lies in the presentation. As most business owners will discover, sometimes during your process of business development you will need to present information about your company, services or products. It may be in your initial process for securing funding or clients. You may be asked to not only develop a proposal, but to also make a presentation. Here is where I have seen the river part between the professionals and the amateurs. Here is the key to any presentation:

"tell them what you are going to tell them, tell them again
&
then tell them you told them!"

This sounds simple, however, I've had to sit through some very grueling presentations. Whether it is the presentation or the presenter, paying attention to the details may be the turning point as to whether you close the deal or not. If you are not the greatest speaker, or presenter, then it will be important for you to find someone else to present the information on your behalf. This may mean working with a professional presentation maker to capture the message you want to tell. The most common mistake I see in presentations is putting too many details, or too much information on one page. Consequently, the main message is lost while the audience is either straining to read the information, or checking their mobile devices for more pertinent information than your presentation.

When it comes to actually making the presentation: practice, practice and more practice! Get others to listen to your presentation at different stages and to ask tough questions to help you develop the information you need to own your presentation. When you formally present, work to avoid reading everything straight from your presentation. If you have to read it, then why as a customer should I believe that you know what you are doing?

In preparing for a presentation, consider getting a coach or mentor to help you with the details. I have been asked by major corporations and organizations to do presentation training since it is not one of those things that everyone does well. We all have read that public speaking is one of the greatest fears that most people face. It is not so much the public speaking that concerns most people, as it is the fear of rejection. This is why soliciting, and receiving feedback, as well as coaching can prepare you for potential questions, including those that may lead to rejection of your proposal.

Review your presentation for spelling errors, or information that may reflect a lack of focus on the details. Check the quality of the printed materials to ensure that pages are numbered and in order. This may sound minor, and yet these are the details that communicate to potential clients that you are not up for the opportunity. Remember the experience that Astrid and I had in preparing for a presentation. It is important that you take time to sweat the details.

Another detail to "sweat" is preparing for the technology glitches that always tend to crop up just when you have your big presentation moment. If you are using a flash drive, ensure you have an up-to-date backup of your files (and a backup to the backup). You may want to send your presentation electronically to a contact in the organization of a prospective client prior to your presentation. You can always lock the presentation to avoid any potential misuse of your information.

Bring paper copies of your presentation for each participant. Although I am not advocating killing trees, I do advocate being prepared. That detail reflects that you care about your audience's time. This holds true even if you are presenting to a large audience. You can also make your presentation available at your website for participants to download later. This will help in conserving the forest. However, you do want to ensure that you have some key information that you can leave with participants after your presentation, including your key products/services, and how to contact you and your organization.

Bring your own computer when possible. Even if you choose not to use it, bringing your computer communicates that you have some technology knowledge, a critical competency for any business owner to demonstrate in today's marketplace.

Of course, technology can be an asset for any business. In addition to the computer, you will need to have a web presence. Most business owners understand the importance of developing a web presence. Unfortunately, sweating the details for website development is often forgotten. Check your website periodically for broken links (they do sometimes break) or for dated information, misspellings or any other inaccurate information. What experience are your visitors having when they come to your website? The rule of thumb is to avoid any extra click-through requirements to get to critical information about you or your business.

Check the email address(es) of your employees or associates and ensure that they are both professional and current. If you choose to participate in social media, keeping these accounts and responses professional and separate from your personal accounts is also an important detail to sweat. Remember, regardless of what happens in your business, the buck starts and stops with you. If you, or anyone in your organization, misuse technology, it can become a detail detrimental to your success.

There are details in any organization. However, the details of business ownership are ones that can not be overlooked. Unlike large corporations with large legal teams, as a business owner, or entrepreneur, for the most part you will not have access to these types of resources. Leverage the resources you do have for managing the details of your business. The diversity of those details will require you to identify diverse resources with diverse skills and competencies to help you manage the details. The lesson is that you had better sweat these details. What may feel like a minor oversight can result in a major disappointment.

LESSON NINE
You Had Better "Sweat" the Details

1) What details of your business operations do you need help managing? Why?

2) Do you understand which details in your business energize you? Which ones drain you? What actions do you take to leverage your strengths to manage the details of these differences?

3) Of the two customer satisfaction factors, *reliability* and *responsiveness,* which do you need to pay more attention to in meeting your customers' needs?

4) What additional information do you need regarding employment, labor or business tax laws; or regarding interviewing and hiring?

5) Who do you have helping you prepare your taxes and understanding employment reporting requirements? What about other important details?

Reflect, meditate on and/or pray about all of your responses.

LESSON TEN

REMEMBER, "THE AWARD GOES TO" ... YOUR SUPPORTING CAST!

Go home to your family and friends and tell them how much the Lord has done for you and how he has had compassion for you.

MARK 5:19

When I began writing this book, I knew it was important for me to share the lessons I learned in developing my business. As most business owners learn early on with their businesses, entrepreneurship can be very rewarding and yet it can be a lonely existence. Although family and friends provide support, unless they are intimately involved in your business their support can sometimes be limited. Nevertheless, it is important that you remember the value that your family and friends add to your ability to survive in business - make time for your family and friends!

In the story of the demon-possessed man in Mark 5, we learn that after Jesus commanded the demons to leave the man, the man begged to go with Jesus. Instead of allowing the man to go with him, Jesus told him "Go home to your family and tell them how much the Lord has done for you and how he has had mercy on you." (NIV) The key lesson here is to ensure that you can go home and share your blessings with your family and friends. Although it has been a tough journey for me in growing my business, one of the toughest lessons was to learn the value of my family and friends in helping me to grow my business.

One of the most memorable experiences that helped with this lesson came early in the development of my business in September 2002. I had been working on a major proposal, while at the same time working with the business owners that I shared space with to plan an open house. I had agreed to bring some platters and bowls for the hors d'oeuvres and also asked my oldest son Robert to help out as a waiter for the event. He had done this type of work before and I thought it would be a good way for him to help us out in the process.

As I prepared to leave for the office the morning of the open house, I ran back and grabbed several of my most prized crystal bowls and platters to bring to the office. As I packed the crystal in the box, a chill ran through my body that was like a forewarning that this could be the last time I would see the crystal. Thoughts of the crystal being taken by mistake or perhaps stolen passed through my mind. I remember looking at one piece that had been given to me by employees when I left Seattle to move to Charlotte. The piece had been personally engraved with the team's name and had been dedicated to my years of service. I worked to shake the feeling of impending doom and lowered the box into the trunk of my car.

For the majority of the day I was focused on getting the proposal ready to send to the potential client. In fact I was putting the finishing touches on the proposal as guests were arriving for the open house. Robert had arrived earlier and was sitting in my office waiting for me to give him directions for the evening. I asked him to get the crystal from the trunk of my car to give to the caterer.

Continuing to work on the proposal, I didn't notice that Robert hadn't returned. After about 30 minutes Robert returned looking chagrined - I knew immediately that somehow my crystal had suffered a fate that would mean I would never see it again. Business associates ran to my office in response to my screaming and sobbing. I yelled at Robert to leave and not come back. He attempted to explain that the crystal broke when the box slipped out of his hands. With guests arriving for the open house my associates and friends tried to console me. Although I was finally able to regain my composure, the night had been a disaster - close to $3000 in crystal had been reduced to small shards of glass.

As disappointing as the evening had been with me losing the crystal, the more disappointing outcome of the evening was the interaction that I'd had with Robert. Even though I had asked Robert to come and help me, he became the target of my frustration and anger. It wasn't until a year later that I was able to completely reconcile the whole incident.

As we saw in Lessons One and Two, 2003 was the year that I began to understand the importance of working in purpose. It was the year that I found myself physically, financially, intellectually, emotionally and spiritually broke. This was the year that I began to understand what I was supposed to be and what I was supposed to be doing. Night and day I had toiled among things that were like the tombs that the man possessed with demons had dwelled among (Mark 5:5). I was working on projects and proposals that were outside of my purpose and, therefore, were like tombs. It was only when I surrendered to God's will and purpose for my business that I realized that the work I was doing was like chains that I was dragging around.

It was during this period of awakening that I recalled the crystal incident from the previous year. Through reflection on my relationship with Robert, I realized that although he had broken the crystal, it was why he had broken the crystal that helped me to understand the significance of my purpose. The incident actually helped me to *crystallize* my purpose and to have clarity in my work. The incident served as a reminder that my purpose and the purpose of The Galilee Agency was about transformation. I have been called to do work that helps individuals and as well organizations transform to achieve optimal performance. My purpose to help individuals align their spirit and organizations align their culture meant that my being/cause is that of a spiritual advisor. A spiritual advisor not in the sense of a mystical guide or fortune teller, but one whose purpose is to help align vision with mission/destiny. When this is not my primary focus, or primary work, then my outcomes may become shattered like the pieces of crystal that remained in the box that fateful evening in 2002.

A few years after the crystal incident I initiated the discussion with Robert about what I thought happened. Robert acknowledged that he had been angry when I asked him to serve as a waiter. He felt that I did not think enough of his capabilities to involve him in my business. Robert confirmed what I was learning about my purpose and my destiny. At that time Robert was struggling with his purpose and my failure to recognize his spirit helped to create an environment in which we both experienced disappointment.

Even though Robert broke the crystal, I learned not to take the incident personally. Nothing anyone does is about you, it is always about them. Learning to forgive Robert meant I also had to accept my actions as well as to forgive myself, for I was not in purpose that evening. As with other opportunities not aligned with my purpose, the proposal I was frantically working on that evening (in 2002) did not materialize into a contract nor a client. Again, the work was not aligned with my purpose.

The key lesson here is that as entrepreneurs or business owners, we can become so engaged in trying to get that next client or contract that we fail to take time to value those that are most near and dear to us. When working in purpose, we will find that God will provide us with the resources and solutions to help us with our businesses. I have learned that God will help us to remove "chains" that keep us from realizing the possibilities of our businesses. It is, however, important that we value the supporting cast of family and friends so that we are able to share with them the blessings and compassion that God has had for us.

Since that fateful experience in 2002, I have been much more intentional with my interactions with my family. My relationship with Robert has strengthened and deepened as we both have learned to accept each other for our uniqueness and purpose in life. Perhaps the one experience that helped to strengthen my relationship with Robert was the election and inauguration of President Obama. Early on in the campaign, Robert had become an avid supporter. He worked on the campaign and kept me plugged into all of the developments. As it became evident that Obama was to become the 44th President of the United States, I wrote to my representative to get tickets for the inauguration ceremonies in Washington, DC on January 20, 2009.

I was fortunate to receive two tickets to the ceremony. In addition to the tickets, I also received a commemorative invitation and progam. My other son, Rashad could not get the time off from work, however, Robert immediately began to make plans to join me on the trip to Washington. Robert drove from Atlanta to meet me in Charlotte. We left Charlotte that Saturday around noon for Washington. As we traveled north on I-85 and I-95, we saw buses, cars and caravans of cars heading toward the nation's capital for a once in a lifetime event!

Robert and I quickly realized that we were connected not only as mother and son but also as part of a historic event. We spent the weekend with family at my sister Chris' home in Columbia, Maryland outside of Washington. Chris' daughter and my niece, Karren are very involved with the Democratic National Convention. Karren had also been very involved with the Obama campaign from the beginning. She kept us connected with all of the logistical things we needed to know in order to attend the inauguration ceremony.

Chris' daughter, Beverly and her husband Larry had also come from Connecticut; her son Roy and his wife, Karen had come from Texas; and my sister, Mildred had come from Florida. We sang songs, prayed, ate and planned our travel for the morning of the inauguration. Robert and I spent the night before the inauguration at Karren's home which was closer to Washington. Karren left at 4 am and Robert and I left at 5 am. We took the Metro train as we had been instructed by Karren. We were joined by hundreds of others who had come from all over the world for this historic event. Robert grabbed my hand as we ran to hop onto our trains. "Come on Mom," he yelled to me. "You can do it!" With my athletic days far behind me, running to jump on a train was something I had not done for almost 20 years.

Once we arrived at the Capital Mall station, security directed us to the gates according to the color of our tickets. Unfortunately, we had the infamous *"Purple Tickets."* Karren had tickets up front, Mildred and Chris had orange tickets, and the rest of the family had white tickets. If you have not heard by now, those of us with the *purple tickets* were sent to stand in a tunnel to wait until we could enter the gates to the inauguration.

As we stood in the tunnel that cold Tuesday morning we met a woman and her daughters who had come from New Jersey for the historic event. The mother had also stood in the same place years before to hear Dr. Martin Luther King, Jr's "I Have A Dream" speech during the March on Washington in 1962. She had come to the march pregnant. And now, the daughter she was carrying at the time ... had brought her back to Washington. However, like the other thousands of us who stood in that tunnel that morning, the dream was not to be realized for her.

As we entered the tunnel, Robert commented that he did not feel comfortable standing in the tunnel. The bottom line is that we never entered the gates to the inauguration. As the thousands of us left the tunnel we were told that the gates for *"purple"* ticket holders had never opened. The level of disappointment could be seen in the tears of many of those around us. Grandmothers, grandfathers, children and the thousands of us who had stood in below freezing weather that morning for hours stood befuddled and in shock to learn that the gates had never opened.

At one point we saw some of the crowd rushing to jump over the gate. Again, Robert grabbed my hand and we hurdled one gate much like prisoners escaping to freedom! When we arrived at the large gate which was the entrance to the ceremony, Robert wanted to climb the gate. As I contemplated joining him in this endeavor, I looked back at the crowd and knew that if Robert and I tried to climb that gate that morning, disaster would surely follow. Within a few moments, I was able to compose myself and focus on my purpose. I recognized that our actions could have potentially set off a misalignment that could have resulted in arrests or even deaths.

With that, I grabbed Robert's hand and we made our way back through the crowd. It was as if my purpose was calling! Getting through the crowd was not my focus - my focus was on getting to where I needed to go. As we moved upstream through the shocked and disappointed, the crowd began to shout, "Let us in!" Robert and I kept moving until we could faintly hear the shouting.

Another interesting thing about the whole event, as Robert and I made our way out of the crowd, was that there were no police or security officers anywhere to be found. How could this happen with such a historic and major event such as the inauguration of the President of the United States of America? Robert began to ask me where I was going as we pulled each other through the crowd. I had come to witness the inauguration and I was determined that was what we were going to do. Several hotels near the capital had guards standing in their doorways not allowing folks to come into their lobbies to watch the ceremony.

As we pushed past small groups standing in the streets overcome with emotions, Robert and I saw a man standing outside of a small pub. He looked as if he could have been a street beggar. He beckoned to us and asked if we wanted to see the inauguration. He pointed us toward the pub and told us to go inside. Robert and I went into the small establishment and found the place filled with others who were there to see the ceremony. Kelly's Irish Times Pub on "F" Street opened its facility to the "huddled mass" to witness this historic event. The warmth was a welcome relief from the freezing cold that we had experienced for the past six hours.

It was not just the heat we experienced that morning in Kelly's, it was also the warmth we felt in the spirit of those in the cozy establishment. As we witnessed the ceremony that morning in January, those of us who stood and sat in Kelly's that morning were forever connected in history. The team at Kelly remained aligned to their motto, mission, or purpose: *"Give me your thirsty, your famished and your befuddled masses."* Perhaps other establishments should have taken Kelly's approach that morning and remained aligned with their purposes. Consequently, there are some hotels that I will refuse to give my business to as a result of their behavior that morning.

Interestingly enough, when Robert and I left Kelly's that morning we looked for the man who had directed us into the pub. We never saw him again! What Robert and I shared that morning and that weekend was the beginning of a renewed relationship that continues to grow not only as mother and son, but as individuals who understand the importance of remembering that those who hold your hand during the most difficult and challenging times are those who will travel the farthest with you!

As I move through the process of discovering my purpose I have become more intentional with walking in purpose with my supporting cast. I take time to be available to listen to their spirits and to share in their visions. As Robert and I have grown closer in our relationship, I have also watched Rashad grow into "his own man." As I noted, I started The Galilee Agency when Rashad was in his second year in college at Morehouse College. He had already declared his major for business management. One of my concerns was having the financial resources to keep him in college. Although Rashad was a bright student, he had only received minimal financial assistance for college, most of which was for Parent Loans.

I remember Rashad calling me one day to deposit money into his account at school in order for him to buy his books. I had about $30 in my checking account at the time. It was the most difficult message I could give Rashad at that moment. The only thing he could do was to go and put his books on reserve until I figured out where I was going to get money to send to Morehouse. As I drove back to my office from an appointment later that day, I began to pray for an answer. Where was I going to find money for Rashad's books? My cell phone rang and it was Rashad. "Mom," he said, "that was quick." Before I could answer he began to tell me that when he went to put his books on reserve the cashier informed him that he had a $200 credit left on his account. The credit was left after almost $300 had been credited toward the books he was supposed to be putting on reserve.

To this day, Rashad and I have no idea where the $500 came from, we were just grateful that it was there when we needed it the most. He successfully graduated two years later with honors. Nonetheless, what I learned from the experience with the books was that I needed to focus on helping to manage Rashad's education while I focused on developing my business. It was important for me that Rashad focus on his studies and not worry about how the bills were going to get paid. Rashad, however, has always been very enterprising. He has always taken managing his life very seriously. Each semester he always managed to have a part-time job to help with expenses.

Both Robert and Rashad have always been entrepreneurial. Robert was always the more creative and Rashad, more methodical and analytical. I remember when Rashad was only five years old and we were living in Seattle. Rashad handed me his Christmas list that year. He began to develop lists when he learned to write - his nickname used to be "Secretary of State" for his ability to keep track of all of our planned activities, groceries and school supplies. I was surprised to see on the list a "DustBuster." This was the earliest version of the handheld vacuum cleaner used for those small cleanup jobs around the house. The original "Ghost Busters" movie had been released for a couple of years at the time and had a significant commercial following. When I asked Rashad for clarification, he stated just as he had written, "I want a DustBuster!" He was only five years old and certainly I thought he had somehow confused the two titles. I decided that Santa would not bring the DustBuster for Christmas.

So another year came around, Rashad was now six years old, and again the DustBuster was on his Christmas list. The request had also been on his birthday list earlier that year in March. This time I sat down with Rashad after Christmas and asked him why he wanted a vacuum cleaner? In his matter of fact response, he said, "Mom, I need the vacuum to make extra money. I can vacuum your car and other family members' cars." He had the spirit of being an entrepreneur 15 years before I started The Galilee Agency. There were no business owner role models in his life at the time. We were living in

Seattle and my parents had sold their grocery business years before Rashad was born. I was committed to being successful in Corporate America, so where was this enterprising and entrepreneurial spirit coming from? I have to believe that it is part of his destiny. After all, Rashad's middle name is the same as my father's middle name: Marcel.

Rashad continues to be enterprising and is currently developing his own business in Atlanta, Georgia. Warren Enterprises is a multi-level business with its primary presence online. As with Robert, I am very intentional in supporting Rashad with his business development efforts. They both have found ways to support me even when things have been very grim for my business. They are as encouraging of me to keep going as I am of them with their efforts. They definitely deserve awards for their outstanding support!

My parents both passed away before I started my business. My father passed away in 1991 and my mother passed away in 1998. My oldest sister, Mildred, stepped in after my mother passed and continues to be one of my biggest supporters, much like my parents had been even before I started my business! My sister, Dr. Mildred A. Hill-Lubin, is accomplished in her own right. She retired from the University of Florida as a professor of african literature. She has traveled all over the world and has students from all over the world. Some students from her classes 10-15 years ago still ask her to be a reference for them as they pursue their career and professional goals. With all she has accomplished she continues to tell me how proud she is of what I am accomplishing. Whenever she calls she is always supportive and encouraging, telling me how proud she is to be my sister. In addition to words of encouragement, Mildred has also provided financial support during those times when cash flow was not flowing. She has never asked me to give her a time when I could repay her, and instead has only ever wanted me to keep going.

This is the type of support that I wish for all business owners and entrepreneurs. Furthermore, it is how you remember that support and the cast of supporters that stands with you that makes the difference.

I could not close this chapter without remembering my best friend and life supporter, Maurice Scott! As I have noted, every business owner needs a mentor, coach or someone who can help you see the reality of your situation.

Maurice has been that type of supporter for me. He has been with me from the beginning and has seen me as I have experienced the exciting highs and the awful lows! He has always been the one to ask me the tough questions about some of my business decisions. Sometimes your greatest supporter is also the one that shows you the toughest love. There have been times when I did not want to listen or hear what Maurice had to say. At times he can be the Simon Cowell of real talk! However, when I look back at Maurice's counsel, it is evident that he has always had my best interests at the center of his feedback. If I could give him an award, it would have to be for Outstanding Performance as Supporter in a major lifetime production!

There are others who have been part of my supporting cast and have helped me along the way. I have learned to be more intentional in remembering my supporting cast. I take time to make calls to check on family and friends. I also take time to have lunch or dinner to renew or energize relationships with those that have been part of my supporting cast. It does not matter how small their support has been, I have learned that I could not have done it without them. It is their concern for my well-being that helps me to understand why I am doing this. I make myself available to remember this support. To achieve this availability I take time for renewal of my spirit. God has been faithful and I have learned to walk in my purpose.

It brings me great joy to share this faithfulness with my family and my friends. As they see what God has done for me and The Galilee Agency, it is my prayer that they begin to learn the importance of being purpose-inspired. It is why I wanted to share these lessons with others who may be asking, "Why am I doing this?"

Regardless of what level of success you achieve in your business, or as an entrepreneur, if you do not take time to remember your supporting cast, are you truly successful? If a tree falls in the forest and there is no one there to see it fall, did it really fall? If you achieve all of your business goals and are recognized for your accomplishments and yet there is no one there to share the story with you, is it truly success?

Take time to remember your supporting cast so that you will be able to go home and tell family and friends how you have been blessed! Remember the award always goes to your supporting cast!

LESSON TEN WORKSHEET
Remember, "The Award Goes To" ... Your Supporting Cast!

1) Who is your supporting cast and what roles will they play, or do they play, in your business?

2) How will you tell that your work is aligned with your purpose?

3) What work or actions will you need to develop to ensure that your business is aligned with its purpose, or your purpose?

4) What actions will you take to demonstrate to your supporting cast that they are valuable to your purpose and/or the purpose of your business?

5) How will you demonstrate that your business is purpose-inspired?

Reflect, meditate on and/or pray about all of your responses.

Epilogue

A True Story!

At the beginning of *From Zero To Faith*, my objective was to provide a guide based on lessons I have learned through being a business owner who has discovered her purpose in life and for her business. The book was designed for other business owners, especially entrepreneurs, or for those of you who are thinking about or planning to start a business. It is by no means an answer to all of the questions, or a solution to all of the situations that you will face in business. It is instead my attempt to help you answer the question of why you decided to go into business for yourself and/or for your family. You may not have had the opportunity to ask this question.

I work with clients who have very established and successful businesses and organizations, and it is a question that even they ask from time to time. Finding the answer depends on how aligned they are with their purpose. You will need to answer that question during the course of your business experience. It is how you answer the question that will make the difference in the outcome.

I have attempted to share information that no one will tell you about being an entrepreneur/business owner. I have shared some very personal accounts about my experiences that most folks are uncomfortable in sharing with others. It is part of my purpose to align others with their purpose, so I can't teach what I don't know or haven't experienced. I can't lead when I don't know where I am going!

Recently I had the opportunity to be in a meeting with an individual who I had worked with several years earlier. I had been an executive coach for him and was helping him to answer some key questions regarding his future with the organization. At the time it was apparent that this individual was not feeling fulfilled and successful in his current role. Although he had experienced a great deal of success in his career and was well known for his community work, it was apparent that his future course was requiring him to rethink why he was doing what he was doing. Once we arrived at his "spirit" or cause, or what he was supposed to "be" doing, it became apparent that his future would mean going outside of the organization to fulfill his purpose.

I had not seen this gentleman since that last coaching session several years earlier. However, I knew that he had become an entrepreneur and had become somewhat successful with his venture. When he approached me after the meeting that day he looked considerably younger than when I last saw him. He grabbed my hand and thanked me for what I had done to help him find his purpose. He smiled broadly as he thanked me for helping him answer the question as to why he was doing what he was doing. By answering that question he began his new career and has never looked back. He now knows that his work is aligned with his purpose.

This is an example of how learning to work from purpose, or learning to be purpose-inspired, can influence what you can do with your business. There are still other critical questions that you will need to answer and other challenges that you will need to address. Understanding your purpose and your being (spirit or culture) will greatly enhance your ability to do what you want to do and/or to achieve your vision or calling. I have organizational clients now that have been able to achieve this alignment. A testament to this alignment is the subsequent robust growth in business and in opportunities for the organization. I have individual clients as well that have been able to achieve this alignment and are also experiencing personal as well as professional growth.

As I put the finishing touches on this book, I had the divine opportunity to meet and hear Mr. Warren Brown. Warren is the founder and owner of CakeLove and Love Café. He currently has seven retail storefronts in the Washington, D.C. metropolitan area.

You may remember Warren from his Food Network television show, "Sugar Rush." If you are not a Food Network fan, you may have heard about Mr. Brown on Oprah or some other major morning news show. Warren left a promising career practicing law to start a bakery in 2002. As fascinating as the story is, it is Warren's story that he told at the Charlotte Chamber of Commerce breakfast meeting a few weeks ago that captured my interest. His story literally spoke to the concept of why finding purpose helps to align you for business success.

In addition to his retail enterprise, Warren Brown has written two books. His first book, *CakeLove* tells the story of his transition to follow his passion that led him to create the CakeLove enterprise. His second book *United Cakes of America* also captures his passion and the passion of others around the United States for baking cakes. As fascinating as these accomplishments are, it was that one story Warren told to our breakfast meeting that basically finished my book!

Warren described an epiphany from a time before he left the law practice to open his first bakery. He shared the story of how late one night he was baking a cake. He was also struggling with how he could leave the law practice and open a bakery. He noted that he was extremely exhausted and yet he wanted to make the best cake he had ever baked. He related that he was making a cake for one of the senior managers in the law office and wanted to ensure that the cake reflected his best work. The cake was crowned with candied navel orange segments. As he carefully placed extra orange segments onto the top of the cake he found himself overwhelmed with emotions.

As he looked at the pattern of the orange segments he remembered a childhood friend. He remembered that this was the friend with whom he learned how to play basketball, football and other sports. As he remembered his childhood friend he also remembered their talks while eating oranges after sport practice or a sporting activity. His friend would always remind him, "Warren, life is for living." Unfortunately, Warren's friend passed away at the age of 17.

During this emotional moment, Warren also began to remember the creative patterns he used to draw over and over with chalk when he was a young boy. The pattern on the cake he was now preparing in his kitchen was identical to those early childhood drawings. Warren realized, at that moment, that baking cakes aligned his future with his past. His ability to let go and go toward his purpose released the emotional struggle he was having with leaving the law practice. His passion for who he is as a baker can be felt in his spirit and in his words. He knew at that moment that his focus had to be on where he was going and not what he was leaving.

As we left the breakfast meeting that morning I shared with Warren the following: "You found your purpose that night. The passion you have for your business is evident in who you are - you are a great example of a purpose-inspired story!"

Warren Brown and the CakeLove story is truly a reflection of purpose-inspired entrepreneurship. When asked if there were plans to expand the business beyond the Washington DC area, Mr. Brown confidently responded that unless he could guarantee that the business remained aligned with who he was, he was not interested in the endeavor of expanding beyond the current geography. His ability to remember and engage with his supporting cast is a source of inspiration for him as well.

Since opening his business, he is now married and has a daughter. Warren Brown is indeed a purpose-inspired entrepreneur, who has come from a place of zero to faith! As Warren Brown discovered his purpose he has aligned his business with it and has been able to sustain his passion. This alignment is evident when you meet him and hear him speak. To learn more about Warren Brown and CakeLove visit http://www.cakelove.com.

Achieving a purpose-inspired alignment requires hard work and some tough lessons that you may need to learn. Sustaining this alignment will also require practice! I have found Don Miguel Ruiz' The Four Agreements[6] as great reinforcing principles and tools for practicing purpose-inspired leadership. Learning to speak with words that help you to move will greatly enhance your ability to move toward your vision. Learning to avoid taking anything personally and making assumptions will help you to choose responses that will keep you aligned rather than reacting to influences beyond your control. Lastly, learning to always do your best will mean that you understand your purpose and, therefore, the work you are doing is also aligned with your purpose. When your work is aligned with your purpose, your capacity to do your best will be enhanced. You will find that you have more passion and your work will be energizing.

As I have noted, entrepreneurship has a long lineage in my family. The history of business ownership goes back to my grandfather and his brother and sisters. When tracing our family history and roots, we discovered that my grandfather's brothers and sisters shared in the family business and

---

6   Ruiz, Miguel. The Four Agreements: A Practical Guide to Personal Freedom. San Rafael, Calif: Amber-Allen Pub, 1997.

were entrepreneurs as well. So it was not surprising that my father and his brothers and sisters became entrepreneurs. One of my paternal aunts owned a restaurant and bar, and another owned and managed several properties in my hometown of Columbus.

The compelling story of entrepreneurship and destiny continues today with many of my family members. Recently, my niece, Rev. Veronica Anderson Lewis shared a profound story regarding her husband's new venture. In addition to leading a church as a pastor, Veronica is also an entrepreneur in the jewelry business. As Veronica and her husband are weathering the economic downturn as so many families are today, her husband, Timothy, started a new entrepreneurial venture. Tim, who is also a pastor and barber, seized an economic opportunity to expand their territory. During the hot summer months in southern Georgia, Tim started selling watermelons growing on his land. Does that sound familiar?

"PaPa had to give us this idea ... I don't even like watermelons," Veronica recounted. "I can feel PaPa showing us how to grow our businesses," she proclaimed. It was as if my father's entrepreneurial spirit was there with Veronica and Tim. As I listened to Veronica tell the story about the watermelons, I had fond memories of my father and the times we spent at the market testing products which, of course, included the watermelons from the southern parts of Georgia.

In addition to Veronica, there are other generations of entrepreneurs in the family. My niece, Janice Tinsley just started a nursing consulting business this year. Another niece Karren Pope Onwukwe is an independent attorney supporting elder care. My nephew, Walter Hill has had the passion of business ownership as long as I have known him. There are many, many more cousins, nieces and nephews who are entrepreneurs, or have achieved their life goals through entrepreneurship. There are, in fact, too many for me to highlight here. Businesses in our family range from developing ventures to very successful enterprises. We have technology, automobile parts, restaurant supply, real estate, insurance, law, education, medical, banking and many other industries represented by entrepreneurs throughout the family. In fact, the family's core values from my father's clan of Anderson–Smith–Howard include "Enterprising and Entrepreneurship."

And, of course, both of my sons, Robert Warren and Rashad Warren, are also entrepreneurs. In addition to working full time jobs, they both have launched their own respective businesses. Robert does entertainment promotion (Cosmic Aliens Entertainment) and Rashad has an online marketing business (Warren Enterprises).

Perhaps there is no one in your family who has been, or ever will be an entrepreneur or business owner. It may, however, still be in your destiny or your purpose to follow your passion and move towards where you need to go. Just like Warren Brown did in 2002, and just like I did in 2001, you will need to listen to that voice calling you toward your purpose to ensure that you are aligned as an entrepreneur or business owner with your purpose.

The lessons I have learned in growing The Galilee Agency have taken me from a place of zero to a place of faith. I have learned that to achieve my vision or calling I had to first understand my purpose, my destiny, and why I am here!

I have learned that in order to fulfill this destiny and to achieve my calling, I have to have a secure foundation of faith, good health, financial resources, a good plan and good support. I know now that you are not in business unless you are making money and that it takes money to make money.

I have learned that many will travel with you, however, only a few will truly be partners with you. It is important to know the difference between those who understand your vision, and your destiny, and those who only want to share in the rewards.

Tough lessons have taught me that not all business is good business and that you will need to ensure that your net is cast well, or rather, that your networking is conducted in the right places with the right people at the right time. With some very painful lessons I have also learned that it is important to build social capital in order to develop your capacity for building true win-win business relationships. Where much is given, much will be required of your time and your resources.

While ensuring that my business and my work are aligned with my purpose, I have learned that there will be those details and business fundamentals that if not managed and operated effectively can be devastating to your business. In fact, one of the major reasons for business failure is the inability to take care of those business responsibilities involving taxation and employment requirements. Failing to take care of these responsibilities will eventually impact your cash flow, and remember, it takes money to make money.

Finally, whatever you learn about why you are owning a business or deciding to begin a business, you will need to know who your supporting cast will be. Most likely your supporting cast will include your family and friends. It will be important that you value their support because they will be the ones that will be proud of your successes and your accomplishments, and they will serve as encouragement when all is not well. As you build your business take time for your family and friends, and especially take time for yourself.

In taking time for yourself you will need to understand your purpose. You will need to be able to find that place that only you and God understand. I believe that your destiny was assigned by Him and that you will need to go to Him to understand it. Practice meditation and listening for His voice or that voice that tells you when you are aligned with your purpose. It may mean finding a quiet place or taking a long walk or drive to listen for that voice that calls you to a place of purpose.

Warren Brown describes a point in which he found himself emotionally exhausted before he finally heard that voice that connected him to his past. Listen for the voice inside, the one that touches your spirit, the one that energizes your work and your actions. When you listen to that voice you will hear and know the answers to the question as to why you are doing this, and you will be able to move from zero to faith.

Go home to your family and friends and tell them how much God has done for you and how he has had compassion for you!

Mark 5:19

ACKNOWLEDGEMENTS

I want to acknowledge and thank my supporting cast of family and friends who have been with me on this journey … especially those who encouraged me to put these lessons into written words.

I want to thank Tana and Mike Greene of Strataforce for being the best marketing representatives that a small business owner could have and, more importantly, for being great clients and friends. The support of the Greenes led to many other supporters including Michelle and Hugh Benjamin of Benjamin Enterprises. I look forward to the time I spend with Michelle and Hugh because of the laughter and friendship that energizes my spirit. Sitting behind my desk in my office is a picture of me with Tana, Mike, Michelle and Hugh. The frame reads "Live, Laugh and Love!" Thank you for the opportunity for me to share all three with you!

To Astrid Chirinos, Jo Washington, Flavia Eldemire and Carole Laughlin, my spiritual sisters, thank you for your support and your love! You met me as I was and decided to join me as partners on my journey! Your faith in me has been immeasurable and I am grateful for the opportunities that we have partnered on, aligning our missions together to make a difference for our clients and for our community!

To Cortney Donelson, thank you for your faith, spirit and the commitment to continue traveling with me on this journey. You are indeed a Godsend and a blessed gift! I hope you know that I treasure what you do to help me and The Galilee Agency continue to be a place of transformation.

To my brothers - Robert, Tommy and Luther - thank you for being big brothers! Your calls, birthday cards and notes mean more to me than you will ever know!

To my sisters - Mildred, Christine and Frances - thank you for all of your support and, most importantly, your prayers! Your calls to check on your "baby sister" continue to lift my spirit and always remind me that I am on the right journey and that you are there for me!

To my best friend and confidant, Maurice, whose love and honesty helped me make some difficult decisions when it has been time to understand the difference between the real and the imagined! Thank you for your practical approach to life and for being the type of friend that a struggling business owner needs!

To Robert and Rashad, my dear sons, thank you for helping me to be the mother that you can be proud of and who can be there for you as you realize your purposes! Thank you for making me proud of the choices you are making! Your support, confidence and love continue to serve as energy that helps me continue to believe in my destiny! (Thank you, Robert, for writing the song "Believe!" - it has become my theme song!)

And a special thank you to my ancestors; my grandfather, Charlie; his brothers and sisters; my aunts and uncles; and to my mother and father for your lives, and for living and walking in your purpose. Thank you for your love and your strength for it continues to strengthen me! I pray that you continue to watch over me and that your spirit of enterprising entrepreneurship continues to dwell within me!

And Thank You God for your faithfulness, for the place of Galilee is truly blessed (Isaiah 9:1)! I am blessed to dwell in your love and favor and to walk in your purpose for my life!

ABOUT THE AUTHOR

Brenda F. Anderson is Co-founder, President and CEO of The Galilee Agency, Inc. in Charlotte, North Carolina. The Galilee Agency is an innovative organizational development consulting and training firm focusing on organizational transformation.

Brenda has more than 25 years of leadership and organizational development experience and is a proven consultant, executive coach, facilitator and community business leader. As a result of her insight, innovation and inspiring leadership abilities she has led international and national organizations toward achieving high performance goals. For the past 10 years Brenda has worked with other business owners and entrepreneurs across the United States inspiring them to develop and to grow their businesses and to ensure that they are each strategically aligned with their individual purpose.

Brenda was named one of the Charlotte Chamber of Commerce 2010 Diversity Champions, and has also received the Charlotte Business Journal's 2006 Women in Business Achievement and 2004 Diversity Catalyst awards. She has numerous certifications and community and civic affiliations.

Brenda is the mother of two sons, Robert and Rashad, and lives in Charlotte, North Carolina.

From Zero to Faith: Real Talk for Real Business is Brenda's first book.

For more information about Brenda and The Galilee Agency's consulting, workshops and organizational development services, please visit http://www.galileeagency.com

BLANK PAGE FOR WRITING

BLANK PAGE FOR WRITING

BLANK PAGE FOR WRITING